Mindfulness

Navigate Daily Life Using the Miracle Science of Health and Happiness

(Mindfulness Meditation and Positive Affirmations to Fall Asleep Instantly)

John Anderson

Published by Rob Miles

© **John Anderson**

All Rights Reserved

Mindfulness: Navigate Daily Life Using the Miracle Science of Health and Happiness (Mindfulness Meditation and Positive Affirmations to Fall Asleep Instantly)

ISBN 978-1-989990-79-7

All rights reserved. No part of this guide may be reproduced in any form without permission in writing from the publisher except in the case of brief quotations embodied in critical articles or reviews.

Legal & Disclaimer

The information contained in this book is not designed to replace or take the place of any form of medicine or professional medical advice. The information in this book has been provided for educational and entertainment purposes only.

The information contained in this book has been compiled from sources deemed reliable, and it is accurate to the best of the Author's knowledge; however, the Author cannot guarantee its accuracy and validity and cannot be held liable for any errors or omissions. Changes are periodically made to this book. You must consult your doctor or get professional medical advice before using any of the suggested remedies, techniques, or information in this book.

Upon using the information contained in this book, you agree to hold harmless the Author from and against any damages, costs, and expenses, including any legal fees potentially resulting from the application of any of the information provided by this guide. This disclaimer applies to any damages or injury caused by the use and application, whether directly or indirectly, of any advice or information presented, whether for breach of contract, tort, negligence, personal injury, criminal intent, or under any other cause of action.

You agree to accept all risks of using the information presented inside this book. You need to consult a professional medical practitioner in order to ensure you are both able and healthy enough to participate in this program.

Table of Contents

INTRODUCTION 1

CHAPTER 1: WHAT IS MINDFULNESS? 6

CHAPTER 2: IMPACTS OF A CLUTTERED MIND 24

CHAPTER 3: HOW CAN MINDFULNESS INCREASE YOUR HAPPINESS 31

CHAPTER 4: HOW TO INTEGRATE MINDFULNESS IN YOUR DAILY LIFE 45

CHAPTER 5: MINDFULNESS FOR BEGINNERS – CONTINUED 59

CHAPTER 6: THOUGHTS AND EMOTIONS 77

CHAPTER 7: MINDFULNESS MEDITATION BASICS 82

CHAPTER 8: HOW TO APPLY MINDFULNESS DAILY 94

CHAPTER 9: WALK THE TALK 99

CHAPTER 10: WHAT YOU NEED TO KNOW BEFORE TEACHING YOUR CHILD MINDFULNESS 105

CHAPTER 11: MINDFULNESS MEDITATION AND BUDDHISM 112

CHAPTER 12: WHAT IS MINDFULNESS? 125

CHAPTER 13: EXERCISES TO REDUCE STRESS AND ANXIETY 130

CHAPTER 14: FREEING OURSELVES FROM IDENTIFICATION 137

CHAPTER 15: MINDFUL MEDITATION FOR COMMUTING STRESS.. 142

CHAPTER 16: MINDFULNESS EXERCISES FOR SELF CONTROL AND EMOTIONAL STABILITY... 155

CHAPTER 17: HOW TO MEDITATE AS A BUSY PERSON... 165

CHAPTER 18: THE HISTORY OF MINDFULNESS 173

CONCLUSION... 183

Introduction

Are you a restless soul? Are you constantly agitated and find it hard to unwind? If you are exhausted and know that you need to slow down, then this is the book for you.

Since the beginning of time, the human mind and behavior have perplexed us. It has been one of life's enduring mysteries.

In the past five decades, however, immense progress has been made in the research of significant variations in personalities. Numerous researchers have published theories offering their analysis of the complexities of human behavior. Most of these may sound like Greek to a layman but in this book, we offer some insight into what is termed 'Type A' behavior.

The term 'Type A' is generally used to refer to the pushy, overly-ambitious workaholic who is ever-conscious of deadlines. On the flip side, that same individual may also be described with adjectives like - Strong. Decisive. Diligent. Goal-oriented. These are all wonderful traits – what this book aims to do is to build on those strengths while offering some tools to help you to work on managing the less popular attributes of a Type A behavior pattern. It will no doubt improve your professional and social interactions and perhaps more importantly, it will reduce your stress and anxiety levels. When you consider that studies have shown that persons displaying Type A patterns are twice as likely to develop coronary heart disease than persons who have a more laid back approach to life, then you realize why it is important to address this issue now.

The techniques that are outlined in this book are straightforward and easy to follow. I make the assumption that the reader is not already exposed to meditation so my approach is to explain why mindfulness provides the perfect framework for the Type A personality to manage their emotions and actions. Then I elaborate on those techniques that are most suited to the needs of my target audience. You will discover that by adopting these simple techniques, you will create a more balanced, and possibly, a longer life.

Mindfulness has been attributed with great success in relieving anxiety and other stress-related maladies. It is training the brain to change its response to stress. These mental exercises restructure the way we think and act; bringing about great improvements in our general health and quality of life.

Through this book you will learn the basic steps involved in mindfulness meditation and discover how to use it as a tool to your advantage. You will learn easy to follow steps which will help you to achieve perfect alignment between your thoughts and actions.

The ancient science of meditation is now being recognized the world over for its life-changing benefits. By following the steps outlined in this book, you too will discover how it can enhance your life and experiences. The pressures and stress will give way to a calmer, happier and more contented individual. Mankind's greatest weapon is our ability to choose our thoughts. Thus, our well-being is in our own hands.

Throughout the book, we refer to the 'Type A individual' or 'Type A person', this refers to someone who displays higher levels of Type A tendencies. As the extensive research of the pioneers in behavioral theory confirm, our 'type' is found at varying points along the scale of behavior patterns, so you may display some Type A characteristics but not others. Choose from the menu provided, those techniques and tips that will be most helpful in the areas in which you want to see improvements and diligently apply those to your life to optimize your results. This is an investment in yourself that you will never regret.

Chapter 1: What Is Mindfulness?

There was a servant who had worked for years serving his master at his beckon call. The master lived in a large mansion but would never leave his room. Whenever he wanted his servant, he would call the servant, who would come to the door of the master's room. The door was always locked so the servant would listen to his master's orders through the closed door. One day, the servant was performing his duties when he saw a maid who also worked at the mansion. The servant shared with the maid how he was becoming more and more displeased with his master. "I have worked for my master for many years, and I do everything he asks me to do, yet he is never pleased. Nothing is ever good enough for him; he always wants more and more." The maid told the servant that he should talk to the master about this and let him know how he felt. The servant thought about what the maid said. He had realized that he had always listened to the master without ever questioning him. He was so frustrated at this point that he decided that he would talk to the master. The servant went to the master's door and called his name, but there was no response. He then knocked on the door, still no response. The servant then turned the doorknob, and the door opened slightly. The servant could not believe it; the door was unlocked. Never before had the door not been locked! The servant gathered his courage and entered his master's room; what he saw left him stunned. His master's room was empty; there was no furniture, no master! The servant stood in the empty room in despair, realizing that he had spent all these years serving someone who did not exist.

The story of the servant and his master represents the essential purpose of practicing mindfulness, which is to become the master of our minds, instead of our minds becoming the master of us. Just like the locked room that contained an illusionary master, our minds are always issuing thoughts to us, which we frequently observe without questioning.

When the Mind Masters Us

When you take a shower in the morning, do you experience the sensations of water gliding across your flesh or are you caught up in your thoughts? When you eat, do you savor the taste and texture of your food or do you just swallow it while being preoccupied with thought? When you walk outside, do you notice the delicate leaves of plants and the way that the sunlight enhances their color, or are you thinking of your "to do" list? When driving, do you notice the way the shadows of the passing cars glide over the pavement? Perhaps these things seem irrelevant to you. Let us consider something more meaningful. When you are with that person that you tell yourself is so important to you, do give them your undivided attention when you listen to them? Or, are you formulating your response to them as they are talking to you? Can you allow another to fully express their sorrow, anger, or fear to you? Or, do you try to make them feel better or attempt to persuade them to see your point of view? Are you aware of thoughts and emotions when they first appear in your awareness? Or, do you just find yourself getting angry, worried, frustrated, or depressed because that is the way you feel? Do you experience the moment to moment magic of life, or is your attitude toward life that it is "just another day"? To live mindfully is to be fully aware of what is happening now, at this moment. When we practice mindfulness we become aware of everything that is happening within us and around us. Our awareness is concentrated on that which we are experiencing in the moment, and we experience the moment with complete openness and acceptance.

When you take a shower, is your mind elsewhere? Have you ever seen two people so engrossed with their cell phones that they do not share eye contact? Have you ever driven somewhere only to reach your destination without any memory of the trip? Have you ever been distracted while eating something, not realizing that you had completely consumed it? These are just a few examples of a lack of mindfulness.

If we are thinking about what to do, what to say, or how to respond, we are not being mindful. If we are trying to deny our experience, we are not being mindful. If we are trying to analyze, evaluate, or modify our experience, we are not being mindful. When we receive all of the experience just as it is, with appreciation and gratitude, we are practicing mindfulness.

Mindfulness is not easily understood by most people unless they have personally experienced it. Trying to explain mindfulness is like trying to express the joys of eating chocolate mousse to someone who has never eaten it. In our busy, fast-paced society, with all of its distractions, most of us spend a significant portion of our lives not living mindfully. We are unaware of life in the present moment as our minds are carrying us off to a different time and place. We get caught up in our thoughts of the past or the future, completely oblivious of life's richness.

Mindfulness is not just a spiritual or metaphysical practice that is engaged in by mystics or seekers; it is both a vital aspect of our happiness as well as being a precious gift that comes with being a conscious being. Without mindfulness, we cannot become fully actualized human beings; rather, we become reactive to situations and events. Instead of using our potential to expand our awareness, we live our lives based on a stimulus-response existence.

All of the societal problems, be it violence, intolerance, poverty, hunger, injustice, or the destruction of the environment are directly linked to our lack of ability to be fully present in our lives. Because we are not fully present, we lack clarity of awareness and wisdom when dealing with the challenges that we face, resorting instead to imposing solutions that are based on habit, fear, expediency, or rushed judgment.

To be fully actualized as a human is to be able to access the wisdom and awareness that is needed to create value, a value that benefits both ourselves and others. This creation of value can only come from being fully aware of what is happening at the given moment, both within us and outside us. Without this awareness, we stumble through life and often create suffering for ourselves and those around us.

Our place in life is intimately connected to all of existence. If you were to pull a single strand of a spider's web, the entire web would experience your pull. Developing mindfulness enables us to respond to life in a manner that takes into account how our thoughts, feelings, emotions, and actions are directly linked to life's web. The quality of our lives is directly proportional to our level of awareness to it.

The Web of Life

Our minds create a sense of separation; however, this is just an illusion. In truth, everything that exists shares the same foundation of existence, which is non-physical in nature. The world of form arises from the formless. Through our eyes, the world may seem to be inhabited by an infinite variety of living and nonliving beings, with each one of them being a separate entity unto itself. One who has cultivated mindfulness sees unity, not separateness. Without rain, the flower could not exist. Rain comes from clouds. Without clouds, the flower cannot exist. The flower depends on sunlight for photosynthesis, so the existence of the flower is dependent on the sun. The soil, which contains nutrients and holds the water for the flower, is also vital for the existence of the flower. The flower is also dependent on the gardener who tends it and looks after its needs, making the gardener also a vital part of the flower's existence. Because the gardener needs to eat, the farm, which supplies the gardener with his food, becomes indirectly vital for the flower's existence. The rain drop, the cloud, the sun, the soil, the gardener, and the farm are just some of the components that make it possible for the flower to exist. In turn, all of these components owe their existence to living and nonliving beings. At an essential level of the universe, the true entity of the flower is the entire universe. If just one "component" failed to exist, then the flower could not exist. From this perspective, the flower contains the entire universe, while providing evidence for the existence of the universe itself.

Masters of Mindfulness

Do you have a dog or cat? Do you enjoy being around animals? Does being with your pet, or around animals, have a calming effect on you? There are a number of reasons why dogs and cats are popular as pets. Your dog does not judge you; your dog has a complete acceptance for who you are. Not only that, your dog fully accommodates whatever is happening at the moment. Unlike ourselves, animals are not preoccupied with what may happen in the future, nor do they dwell on the past, which is not to say that animals cannot anticipate what may happen in the future or have memories of the past. Memories and anticipation may arise; however, animals are not distracted by these mental activities; they are focused on what is happening in the current moment. We love our pets, because they cause us, unconsciously, to experience our own sense of being present, if we allow this to happen. Animals and babies are masters of remaining fully aware of the present moment. Now take a moment to reflect on how you live. How much of your day is spent planning, strategizing, anticipating, or dwelling on your memories?

What Your Focus Says about You

You can always determine what a person values by where they are placing their focus and attention. Most of us will make the noble claim that our spouses, our partners, or our families are the most important thing in our lives. Now think for a moment and be honest with yourself. How much time do you give these people your complete and undivided attention? By undivided attention, I mean that you are not looking at your electronic device; you are not anticipating what they are about to say; you are not formulating a response as they speak to you, and you are not thinking about anything else, including yourself. Most likely, such encounters rarely happen. The sad thing is that this kind of attention is what we all want. We just do not want it; we need it. Which goes back to why dogs are so popular; they give us their undivided attention. Whether we lost our keys or find it difficult to give others our undivided attention, the reason for these and all other challenges that we face, without exception, has to do with thought. Inaccurate memories prevent us from finding our keys and competing thoughts prevent us from giving our loved ones our full attention. But the problem is not thoughts; it is our relationship that we have with them.

Clearing the Minds Waters

Imagine a clear jar filled with water. At the bottom of the jar lies a layer of sand. The jar is shaken and placed on a table. With the aid of a flashlight, a beam of light is directed at the jar. The beam becomes dispersed as it travels through the murky water, reflected by the grains of sand suspended in it. With time, the sand will settle to the bottom of the jar. This time, when the beam of light passes through the jar, it remains sharp and focused. The jar is a metaphor for our mind; the sand is a metaphor for our thoughts, and the beam of light is the metaphor for our awareness. Collectively, the jar, sand, water, and light become a metaphor for mindfulness. The jar that was shaken is a metaphor for a mind that is not mindful while the jar with the clear water is a metaphor for a skillful mind, a mind that has been trained in mindfulness.

Emeritus Professor Katherine Weare writes "Mindfulness involves learning to direct our attention to our experience as it is unfolding, moment by moment, with open-minded curiosity and acceptance (Kabat-Zinn 1996). Rather than worrying about what has happened or might happen, mindfulness trains us to respond skillfully to whatever is actually happening right now, be that good or bad. This includes paying close attention to inner states such as thoughts, emotions, and physical sensations, as well as to what is happening in the outside world" (Weare, Katherine 2014).

The practice of mindfulness involves learning to focus our attention on that which we are experiencing, at the moment that it is occurring, with a mindset that is open and accepting. To be mindful means to be aware. It means to be aware of the ebb and flow of thoughts, feelings, and sensation within us as well as the activity and objects that are around us. It is to be aware of the words and actions that we unleash and their effects on us and others.

When we are not mindful, we create suffering for others and ourselves.

When We are not Mindful

Most of humanity is not mindful. Our mind's water is murky with thoughts, thoughts of the past and the future. We are unaware of the feelings and emotions' arising within us until it is too late. The undetected feelings and emotions infiltrate our minds and become the filter through which we experience the world and ourselves. Emotions are like tinted sunglasses, but we do not know that we are wearing them. Thoughts also act like tinted sunglasses. Our troubled thoughts, feelings of fear, or emotions of anger, color our experience of life. Conversely, when we experience thoughts of compassion, feelings of caring, and emotions of love, this becomes our experience. By practicing mindfulness, we can train our mind to become aware of the rising and falling of thoughts, feelings, and sensations, so that we are not caught off guard by it. Because they are aware of these phenomena, they respond to moment to moment situations with wisdom.

The person who is unskilled in mindfulness does not understand that they are the cause of all their sufferings. Problems occur because we have not learned to see clearly. We are unaware that we are wearing our tinted sunglasses or that our water is murky. Because we do not see clearly, we fail to respond correctly to situations. Additionally, we are unaware of the connection between our action, or lack of action, and their ensuing effects.

Examples of Mindfulness Practices

Methods for practicing mindfulness are unlimited as to practice mindfulness simply means being aware of experience. Some of the more common practices include:

Focusing on your breathing as you inhale and exhale. Through rhythmic breathing, you can learn to control your autonomic nervous system as well as enhance mental focus and self-awareness. Even small children can be taught mindful breathing by simply having them place a small stuff animal on their stomach as they lie on the floor. The child is then instructed to watch the stuffed animal as it rises and falls with the movements of the abdomen, during breathing.

Learning to be aware of those momentary experiences that are normally overlooked, such as hairline cracks in the sidewalk or the individual leaf of a tree.

Being aware of the transient nature of thoughts and emotions and coming to the realization that they do not define who you are.

Being aware of the coming and going of sensation. Noticing that while you experience sensations, awareness remains untouched by it or any other experience.

Doing body scans where you use your attention to scans your body from the tip of your toes to the top of your head, during which you allow yourself to experience any and all sensations without judgment.

Taking an object of food, such as the raisin, and exploring it with deep attention, experiencing it with all of your senses.

Walking meditation, where the person places their focus on the sensations of walking, placing his or her attention on sensations of the foot touching the ground and the leaving of it.

Learning to focus on extending love and compassion toward other people, including strangers. This practice does not involve any overt acts; rather, it is the experiencing of the feelings of love and compassion for another. This practice begins with focusing on someone you know and then extending it to strangers, and then ultimately to all beings.

Chapter 2: Impacts Of A Cluttered Mind

A chronically cluttered mind will have a major impact on your life, physically, mentally and emotionally. You may not even realize the effect it is having until you release some of this clutter. Basically, you are not seeing the forest through the trees.

Let's take a look at the physical impact first. It is often hard to relate your physical health to your mental state. Modern medicine has trained us to avoid seeing how our mental state affects our physical body, and we assume that any physical ailments we have are stand-alone problems.

In reality, our brain and body are deeply interwoven. You cannot separate one from the other. A great example of this is stress. We often think of stress as a mental thing. We feel stress from work and from keeping a tight schedule in our households. This stress makes us tired and unfocused, but it also wreaks havoc on our bodies. Stress raises hormones like cortisol, which cause us to stress eat and gain weight. It raises our blood pressure and creates problems within the heart if left unchecked. It also affects our digestive system, creating problems like Irritable Bowel Syndrome (IBS) that are generally thought incurable by modern science.

Early physical symptoms of stress are largely ignored. Minor aches and pains can be explained away by sitting too long or sleeping on something wrong. In reality, stress creates an inflammatory response in the body which causes pain in joints and muscles. It is a physical manifestation of stress. It is a real thing, something that science is just beginning to pinpoint.

The inflammatory response caused by stress causes the immune system to respond. Every time we need to use our immune system to deal with this low-level inflammation, it is taking away resources used to protect the body from environmental threats like bacteria and viruses. Symptoms of stress can simply cause you to get sick more often.

As chronic stress continues, the immune system gets tired and weak. It begins to recognize similarities in harmful substances and body cells. Since it can't tell the difference, the immune system begins to attack healthy body cells, causing autoimmune diseases. This is the case in diseases like rheumatoid arthritis, multiple sclerosis and thyroid disorders like Hashimoto's. It has been scientifically proven that stress exacerbates symptoms of Lupus, another autoimmune disease. Stress is real, and it all stems from a cluttered mind.

It is difficult to grasp how mind clutter can affect the body physically, at least until science proves it. It is very easy to recognize how a cluttered mind affects us mentally, emotionally and spiritually, however.

Mental clutter keeps us from living in the here and now. When the mind is consumed thinking about problems and reliving old emotions, you are not present in the current moment. Have you ever pulled out of your driveway and pulled into the parking lot at work, only to realize you don't remember the trip? Your mind knows the way to work, basically puts the present on autopilot, and slips back into thought. Maybe you are still ruminating over that odd comment your spouse made or thinking of how your day is going to go today. Either way, you are too busy with these thoughts to focus on the present moment.

What is the harm in that? Neglecting to live in the moment means you will be missing out on the natural interactions that happen around you. On your ride in, you missed the colors of the sunrise in your rearview mirror, missed that cloud that looked like a bunny soaring high above you. You unwittingly cut someone off, putting another driver in a bad mood for the rest of the day. You are not present. You are not living your life.

The pressure of this life we live means that we are always waiting for the next moment to happen. We are not engaged in the now because we don't feel we have time to let it play out. Have you ever rushed a conversation with someone because you had things to do? Was it really that important that you could not focus on this person for just another thirty seconds? Did you stand there listening for that thirty seconds but didn't really hear them? What is the point?

How about technology? How often do you skip interacting with someone because you are on the phone, or scrolling through social media? Keep in mind that your inner spirit, the force that drives you, existed long before the invention of social media. It thrives on interaction with others, with movement and physical progress. It does not understand the draws of social media.

You are killing your spirit by skipping out on interactions in real life in exchange for this pseudo-world we have built around ourselves. Do you really even know those "friends" you have on social media?

Living in this day and age makes us emotionally numb. Avoiding interactions at all costs means that we are not really using our emotional intelligence. Unless you are fully engrossed in how something makes you feel, you are not actually living. You are not seeing the subtle nuances of life that bring you happiness, joy and a reason to live. The small interactions and appreciation we have at any given moment are what life is all about, and we are missing it!

Take some time to really hear what someone is saying to you. Give your undivided attention and understand the world that is going on around you. Let the past be in the past, and let it go. Hold no grudges, don't let the past define you. And don't worry so much about the future. You don't know what it holds, so there is no sense trying to plan it to a tee. Nobody truly knows how much time they have left, so spending it planning a future you will not have is a true waste. Instead, be thankful and live in the here and now. It is the only thing that is actually real. Everything else is just a figment of your imagination.

Chapter 3: How Can Mindfulness Increase Your Happiness

Have you ever seen people in motion without progress? Most of the times, when people attempt to take an inventory of their lives at the end of a day, a month, or a year, they find that the days, months, and years just flew by just like any other would. They have no tangible things that they can point to as something that has contributed meaningfully to their happiness. Can anyone be truly happy under such circumstances? Hardly. One of the things that are lacking in their lives is mindfulness.

Check out the activities of your own life. Do you find yourself moving purposelessly and automatically through life? Do you react impulsively to people and situations in life? If your answer is yes, then you might not be as happy as you deserve to be. Too bad we're rather too mindless than mindful with life issues to get what we deserve.

That's why dozens of hours are blown away each week in front of the TV, computers, and other modern gadgets. A lot of money is being spent on mindless shopping. All these are both factors and indicators of unhappiness in life.

That's why this chapter is being devoted to the relationship between mindfulness and happiness. To drive home the point being discussed in this chapter and the next, a lot of consideration is given to the opinions of great minds from reputable world-class citadels of learning and of people who have left deep tracks on the path of history.

Consider the position of Martin Seligman, a teacher at the University of Pennsylvania. He posits that happiness does not come to us automatically, but we have to choose to be happy, we consciously strive at it. Doesn't that smack of mindfulness? In essence, he is saying that it is by being mindful that we multiply our opportunity to choose what will make us happy from a long list of options.

Kirk Brown and Richard Ryan of Virginia Commonwealth University and the University of Rochester respectively, collectively summarize in their writings on self-regulation that mindfulness makes you happy because it allows you to be open or receptively aware of what's taking place around you in the present moment. The attention you give to that produces an "observant stance," which in turn increases your self-awareness and gives you more chances to control your feelings and actions. This is a top secret of happiness.

William James, in his book Talk to Teachers, strongly advocates for paying attention to whatever we're doing. Advancing his argument, he says we have to maximize our energy and keep focused if we must reach the potentials we have to live a good life.

Agreeing with that position, Mihaly Csikszentmihalyi from the Claremont Graduate University recommends that gaining control over our willful attention affects our feelings. It makes our lives either miserable or happy. He further suggests that most people are not making optimal use of their minds. Their minds have a higher capacity to process more information than they're allowing to be processed. According to Csikszentmihalyi, we're going to be truly happy only if we consciously focus our energy corresponding to our goals, so that we can enjoy maximum experiences or flow in our lives.

Matthieu Ricard also agrees no less, saying, "It is the mind that translates good and bad circumstances into happiness or misery. So, happiness comes with the purging of mental toxins, such as hatred, compulsive desire, arrogance and jealousy, which literally poison the mind. It also requires that one cease to distort reality and that one cultivate wisdom."

What do all of the above opinions amount to? From the above points, you can deduce four ways in which mindfulness can boost your happiness.

It Can Take You Out Of The Negative Thought Circle

What usually prevents us from being happy is the mind's propensity to drift away into the vain circles of negativity. The mind tends to dwell excessively on present worries, anxiety for the future, an ugly past, or even self-condemnation. This idleness of the mind can drag us into a downward spiral and can blight our lives. Mindfulness employs meditation that rigorously trains your mind, with the goal of making it more familiar with its nature and enabling it to be quicker in observing when it's dwelling on a destructive pattern of thought.

Having this training, our minds can be quite skillful in disengaging from negative thoughts that pull us down, and shift the attention to positive thoughts that up-build. This will assist us in exploring other potentials, in order to attain greater happiness in life. We've thus gained mastery over our mind rather than being enslaved by it. You'll be able to cut short the negative thinking before it completely robs you of your happiness, as you direct your attention to some physical activities.

Here's how William James summarizes it, "The greatest weapon against stress is our ability to choose one thought over another."

Mindfulness Makes You Happier When You Stay Connected

By our very nature as humans, we thrive best when we're in an enjoyable relationship. The neurons in our brain are designed to interact and to flourish during interactions. Alzheimer's disease and mental disorders, in addition to cardiovascular disease, have been linked to loneliness as a factor. As we discussed on page 9 of this book, mindfulness can help us foster helpful relationships, improve interactions, and stay connected. By so doing, it is making us happier, since people flock around us and promote a state of well-being.

Again, experts take sides with this position. One of them is Jim Rohn, who says, "The greatest gift you can give someone is your attention."

It Gives You Contentment

The external forces can make another Oliver Twist of us, luring us to think that our happiness emanates from what we possess. We can be caught up in a web of wanting to acquire more and more money, success, popularity, pleasure, and material success. Yes, you'll be happy as you attain each of these. Nevertheless, such happiness is transient and it will quickly vanish, because its base depends on external factors that we can't control.

However, the great philosopher Aristotle proposes another form of happiness and well-being, which he called eudemonic happiness. Unlike hedonic happiness, which comes from outside, eudemonic happiness comes from within. It's a product of an inner sense of well-being and aligning one's life to one's values. Isn't that what mindfulness is all about?

Mindfulness gives you contentment coming from the fact that you can be aware of factors of happiness in and around you, without the material possessions. This feeling is rare in this era of consumerism. Mindfulness shows you how to be happy any time, at any moment.

On this, Lao Tzu has this to say, "Be content with what you have; rejoice in the way things are. When you realize there is nothing lacking, the whole world belongs to you."

It Assists You To Cultivate Gratitude

A mindful person usually slows down to observe the present moments he finds himself in, as we have discussed. How does this boost happiness? You will be able to connect with what is happening from moment to moment. Doing that makes you aware of the things that are present in your environment and things that you already possessed and achieved. You can but be grateful for what you have. Mindfulness shows you what you have, and that fills you with wonderment, and at times, with awe. This springs up spontaneous gratitude and you're happy for having what you have.

For instance, have you ever done a mindful meditation on the miracle involved in your breathing process? What about your sense of taste and other four senses? Mindfulness can enable you to be grateful for something as simple as the ability to eat your simple meal and drink 'ordinary' water. When you consider, with mindfulness, things that we often take for granted, your happiness will know no boundaries.

Thoughts of several great people bear semblance to this fact. Eckhart Tolle expresses his opinion on this point this way, "Acknowledging the good that you already have in your life is the foundation for all abundance."

How Mindfulness Can Boost Your Focus

Reading this eBook up to this point should have caused your hearts to be brimming with mindfulness practices, mindfulness benefits, and all that you can think of in the field of mindfulness. Wait a moment, please. There's more to it than meets the eye. Read about how mindfulness can boost your focus before you start.

You'll not be quick to forget the top 5 mindfulness practices we discussed on pages 9 and 10. Taking a critical look at those tips will let you conclude that such practices can boost your focus. Still, let's show you how introducing mindfulness practices into your life will fill your day with focus.

Let's say, for instance, that you choose to take a walk in the morning. It doesn't matter whether another form of exercise is included or not. The important thing is that you are able to start your day and stay focused. At that moment, you're not involved with the modern distracting gadgets that keep you from being focused. Your focus is then given a boost as you keep up this practice.

If you mindfully decide to take different routes to work or to places you go to regularly, your focus will be challenged. The same will be achieved if you try to change your parking area. If you use one parking space today and use another tomorrow, your focus will be better while doing it. And if you commute to work via public transportation, you could get off a stop before your actual bus stop. You will be able to learn to focus on taking different routes to work, to focus on learning distinct features of different parking lots, and to focus on ways to and from different bus stops.

From your mindfulness skills, you've learned not to start your day with reading emails and messages from social platforms. Really, what do such things do for you when you allow them too much space in your day? They only distract you and waste your time. However, you become more focused when you've made it a habit to encourage people to visit or call you if they need your attention. Mail and messages will then be used sparingly, and when necessary. Yes, it won't go down well with people initially. But they'll soon come to appreciate your policy of staying focused and following a schedule.

Mindfulness assists you to increase your focus on people and not only on things. As you practice mindfulness, you'll learn to stay in touch with people. You will learn how to make new friends, while not despising the old ones. Focusing on people, you'll learn about their personal lives, and not just about their jobs. You will know about their family and things they believe are important to them. The next time you'll do something together, you'll be able to focus on their person. That's the beauty of mindfulness.

As mindfulness cultivates the true leadership qualities in you, you will get to be more focused on the burning issues and problems. Mindfulness teaches you that everyone who wants to see you certainly needs something—advices, directives, change, and so on. By the time you bring yourself to identify what they truly need, thanks to mindfulness, your ability to focus will have received a boost.

Let the other people have their say; don't be quick to interrupt, but allow them to interrupt you. Try and see the issues at hand through their eyes. Listen to them as if you're being advised through that discussion, and as if you have something to gain there. Resist the urge to be searching your mind for the solutions to the issues you're confronted with before you get the whole picture. All of these fine habits are the ingredients for that increased focus that you'll get from mindfulness.

Chapter 4: How To Integrate Mindfulness In Your Daily Life

People can integrate mindfulness in their daily lives. There are many things that they can do in order to do mindful living. This chapter will discuss tips on how to integrate mindfulness in your life so that you can live with peace in your inner self.

Important Mindfulness Toolset

Living a stress-free life is easily achieved in mindfulness. However, how do you start doing mindful living? Are there things that you have to do in order to adapt this concept in your life? Below are the mindfulness toolset that you need to know to start imbibing peace and self-awareness within you.

Meditation: This is the first step to mindful living. It is not complicated to meditate and all you need to do is to stay still (sit or lie down) for three to five minutes a day. While meditating, focus your thoughts and attention to your body and breathing. This will prevent you from entertaining unnecessary thoughts in your head.

Be awake: Being awake is more challenging than meditation because it requires your mind to stay awake and not wander on thoughts that are unnecessary such as stressing about the future or being immersed in the online world. Being awake is being able to keep your focus for the entire day as you do your tasks.

Watch your urges: It is important that you watch your urges because they can prevent you from losing your focus. Urges give birth to addiction which can prevent you from putting your focus on yourself. Keep your urges in check such as using social media or eating too much.

Let go of your ideals: All of us have ideals but the problem is that the world is never an ideal place and that we are more prone to failing than achieving our ideals. It is important to know that ideals really do not come true so that we can easily let go without the fear of grieving over them.

Accept life as it is: Stop trying to change people to make your life better. It is important that you enjoy what life throws you and accept every situation as it is. The soonest we stop fighting against life, the more at peace we become.

Let go of your expectations: Just like having ideals, we are also prone to make a lot of expectations over things that we will be experiencing. Whenever things do not meet our expectations, we end up feeling stressed and disappointed. The thing is that we are the only ones causing our pain so let go of expectations if you think that they are causing you too much burden.

Embrace discomfort: Not everyone is willing to embrace discomfort. This is the reason why people get stuck with their bad habits. The thing is that most people would rather stick with their bad habits because they know that they will be comfortable. Embrace discomfort and a lot of good things will happen to you.

Watch your resistance: When you do something uncomfortable, you become suddenly resistant to embrace change. It is important that you watch your resistance so that you do not lose your concentration while practicing mindfulness.

Be curious: Let go of what you think that you know and be curious with everything that surrounds you. How will you be able to try things if you are not curious? So let go of what you know and enjoy the benefits of curiosity. After all, curiosity is all about self-discovery.

Be grateful: The problem with most of us is that we complain on just about everything. Remember that life is miracle so there should be two or more things that you can be grateful for. By doing so, you will be able to live a happier and more contented life.

Let go of your control: People want to take control of their lives but the thing is that control is something that we do not have. Entropy is the rule of nature which means that everything will lead to disarray. Life is basically uncontrollable and if you try to control all aspects is your life; you end up getting disappointed and frustrated about everything.

Always be compassionate: Showing compassion for other people can change the way you feel towards yourself and towards the world. If you do it in a daily basis, you will appreciate how it is to live freely.

Meditation Practices for Mindful Living

Meditation is key if you want to bring in more mindfulness in your daily life. It is still important that you incorporate meditation at least a few minutes of your life each day. This section will discuss about the different meditation practices that you can do for mindful living.

Seek guidance from a meditation guru: Meditation does not come naturally for everyone thus if you are still starting with meditation, it is important that you seek guidance from a meditation guru to help you get started. Look for workshop or retreat to ensure that you get the essential foundations to practice meditation correctly.

Find the right technique: There are different ways to meditate and these include yoga, taichi or qi gong. It is important that you explore the different types of meditation techniques so that you can benefit from it fully. As soon as you find the meditation that you want to practice, stick with it so that you can enjoy mindful living.

Follow a schedule: Perhaps one of the biggest mistakes people do when meditating is that they try to squeeze meditation anytime during the day. The problem is that other activities might pop up that can result to you sacrificing meditation. It is important that you stick on a regular schedule and increase your duration as time goes by. The best schedule for meditation is early morning but you can choose any time of the day as your regular schedule just make sure that you stick with it.

Look for a good meditation environment: Set up a space inside your house where you can meditate and relax. Make sure that the area does not come with any clutter, noise, bright lights as well as other distractions that can rob you of quality meditation. You don't need to decorate your meditation room elaborately. Instead, make sure that the space where you are going to meditate in a quiet and comfortable place.

Remove distractions: It is important that you remove all distractions while meditation. However, you cannot control everything that happens in your environment so instead of removing external distractions, you need to remove your internal distractions. Develop the attitude of accepting things as they are. If there are disturbances, let them linger but deal with your internal distractions.

Meditate with someone: Meditation is also more meaningful if you practice it with your friends. Having meditation partners can provide you with the support that you need to keep on tract. Moreover, the commitment that you and your friends share ensures that you and your friends will continue practicing regularly.

Join a meditation retreat: Joining a retreat is very important because it allows you to experience full mindfulness experience. There are different meditation retreats that you can join from afternoon getaways to week-long retreats. The meditation retreat can also vary depending on your capacity. If you want to get away from everything and experience full mindful living, make sure that you join a memorable meditation retreat in your area.

Understand your reasons for meditation: We often get fired up the first time we do meditation. However, our enthusiasm usually wanes after a few months of years of practicing meditation. Staying committed with meditation can be difficult but it is important that you always remind yourself of the any reasons why you started meditating in the first place.

Bring your meditative mentality wherever you go: Meditating allows you to bring out greater degree of mindfulness. The thing is that meditation does not only revolve inside your mediation nook. Take your meditative mentality wherever you go.

Ways to Bring More Mindful Living in Your Life

Living a mindful life can be challenging to begin with. Most people believe that one needs to spend most of their lives meditating and doing yoga. In the previous section, people are encouraged to bring meditative mentality wherever they go. This means that doing simple tasks can be used to create meditative mindfulness. Below are examples of tasks wherein you can incorporate your meditative mentality wherever and whatever you do.

Practice one minute meditation: You don't need to spend a lot of time to meditate. In fact, you can take short meditations throughout the day. Set a timer for 1 minute and focus your entire attention only on your breathing. You can close your eyes while meditating but make sure that you do not lose in touch with your breathing but if you do get lost in your breathing, let go of your thought and bring your attention back to breathing. You can meditate anytime of the day.

Do mindful listening: Connecting to other people is also another goal of mindful living. When listening to other people, it is important that you listen to what they are saying. Focus your attention on the person whom you are conversing with instead of mentally agreeing or disagreeing with what they are saying.

Do your chores as mindfulness sessions: Consider your household tasks as part of your mindfulness session. So instead of thinking about how boring cleaning the bathroom or washing dishes is, use your time as a mindfulness ritual. For example, while doing the dishes, do not rush things through for the sake of getting things done. Notice and feel the texture of the china and the water flowing as you wash the dishes. By being mindful with your chores, it will become a sacred ritual that helps you keep in tune with the moment.

Eat mindfully: Eating mindfully can also help you appreciate what you are eating. Moreover, it has also been shown to help people with weight loss issues. So when you sit down to eat your meal, turn off all the things that distract you and just focus on eating. Pause before eating and eat small bites from your food. When you do mindful eating, you easily notice the scent, flavor and texture of food.

Learn to slow down: The problem with our culture today is that we are so busy racing against time that we do not know how to slow down. If we live fast-paced lives, we end up not enjoying the precious things in our lives. By physically slowing down, we also slow down our thoughts thus we get more pleasure out of life because we can do more important things such as connecting with our family.Take one thing at a time: Many people enjoy doing multitasking and they boast about this capability. However, multitasking does not make you productive but it drains your energy faster. The thing is that multitasking does not make you productive only busier and mentally as well as physically exhausted. Instead of doing multitasking, try to focus your attention to one thing at a time. Take each task with full awareness so that you do not make mistakes and forget details. If you take one thing at a time, you end up more efficient without feeling worn out.

Watch your mind: Always watch your thoughts by listening to your inner voice. As you learn how to listen to your mind, you think about your decisions first before becoming too reactive with whatever situation that you are in.

Embrace your idle time: Our culture frowns upon people who "waste" their time by being idle. In fact, many people feel guilty when they sit for a long time doing nothing. Mindful living lets you embrace idle moments. However, you need to use your idle time to listen to yourself. Position yourself in a comfortable spot and be still. Bring your awareness to the present moment to improve your sensory perception. So the next time that you have nothing to do, use it for mindful living.

Mindful walking: Walking does not only help promote good health but you also give yourself extra time each day to do mindful living. So whether you are strolling in the park or walking from your house to work, you can turn this activity as a form of meditation. To do mindful walking, be conscious of your breathing and the movement of your feet.

Moreover, pay attention to the details on your surroundings. So when you are walking, walk as though your feet are kissing the Earth. Only when you learn to appreciate what is around you will you be able to turn this activity into meditation.

Use your urges: All of us have cravings, urges and even addictions. You can use them as a wakeup call so that you can do mindful living. When you feel that you need to do an urge, use this feeling to bring awareness into yourself. For instance, if you feel sensations of craving, acknowledge the presence and notice if the craving provides physical sensation to the body. If it is, aim your mind to remain in the "present" so that you don't give in to your urges but is able to use it for mindful living.

Chapter 5: Mindfulness For Beginners – Continued

Like I said earlier, mindfulness is not something exotic and meant only for those who choose to live the life of a hermit. It is a form of practice to bring to the fore the natural ability of the mind to be in the present moment. We can practice mindfulness in everything we do including eating, walking, working, conversing, etc. Let us look at each of the day-to-day routines and find ways to become more mindful of our routine activities.

Practicing Mindfulness While Eating

In addition to helping you become more aware of your daily activities and of yourself in general, there are plenty of studies that prove mindful eating practices are great for people who are watching their weight and bad eating habits. One of the primary reasons for overeating is consuming food mindlessly and without thought into what is on our plate. The following mindful eating habits will help you overcome mindless eating habits while helping you become more aware of yourself.

Chewing Your Food Well – This is, perhaps, the easiest and the most effective way of eating your food in a mindful manner. Some experts recommend that you have to chew your food 25 times before you swallow it! While this might seem like to be rather a lot to ask, with practice, it is easily possible to chew the food in your mouth at least 20 times before you swallow it completely. Another big motivation to do this is there are multiple studies proving food intake becomes less when chewing increases.

Use Your Non-Dominant to Eat – An effective way to focus on what you are doing in a more intense way than before is to enhance the difficulty in the activity. For example, if you are right-handed person naturally, choose to eat with your left-hand. This will ensure you are paying more attention to your eating as the activity will not happen naturally and every action will have to be deliberately followed to get it right.

Yes, this is not going to be easy. Yet, you can start small. For example, if you take about 15 minutes to eat your lunch, initially, using your non-dominant hand in the first 5 minutes. Slowly, you can increase the duration. There is a catch here, though. If you become very good at eating with your non-dominant hand, with sufficient practice, you could slip into eating mindlessly again. So, it is important that you find your balance.

Try To Identify All the Ingredients in the Meal — Focus on every bite and try to identify all the ingredients in all the dishes of the meal. Focus on the texture of the food, the taste, the smell and the flavor. When you eat your first bite with focused attention on all the elements of the meal, you will notice yourself eating slowly and trying to identify all the tastes and textures you found in the first bite. Savor your meal.

Eat From a Plate and In Silence – While eating from a plate seems obvious, what I am trying to tell you is to serve the food or the items you want to eat onto a plate and avoid trying to eat straight from the packet. Eating from a packet does not allow you see what and how much you are eating. Transferring it to the plate will help you see the quality and quantity of food you are consuming.

Eating in silence is also very important for mindful eating. Turn off the TV, keep your mobile away, and turn off all distractions that can take your focus off from the meal in front of you. While it might seem very difficult to eat an entire meal without saying a word, you can start off with an attempt of keeping at least the first 5 minutes this way. Slowly, with patient practice, you will find yourself eating in silence.

Focus on the Lifecycle of the Food on Your Plate – In modern times, nearly all of us are disconnected from the source of our foods. We don't know how the food reaches the supermarket. In fact, with increasing dependency on ready-to-eat foods, which only require heating up in a microwave oven, many of us don't even know how food is prepared.

Focusing on the lifecycle of the food on your plate is an excellent way of mindful eating. It is a way of connecting with the world around us. If you pause to think of the farmer who first sowed the seed, how he nurtured the crop, how the crop was harvested, transported, cleaned and packed, and then finally reached the shelves of the supermarket, you will appreciate the food on your plate better as you will see how many people were involved in the entire process.

You will begin to feel a sense of gratitude for the meal on your plate. Eating mindfully and in a manner that is appreciative of everyone's efforts is a way of expressing this gratitude.

Practicing Mindfulness While Walking

Before you begin your walking regimen, find the right place to practice mindful walking. You can choose any place including an outdoor area or an indoor place like your living room too where you can walk back and forth. Mindful walking can be done in a formal way like how you do mindful breathing, or it can take on an informal stance. The common thread that runs through any activity done mindfully is being acutely aware of all elements in the concerned activity.

When we allow our mind to its own devices, it invariably becomes distracted and flits around from thought to thought decreasing your sense of engagement with the activity. When we are mindfully walking in the park or in the living room or between floors, we are removing the autopilot mode of our mind and actually driving it to focus on the present moment. Here are some tips for mindful walking:

Walk at a natural pace with your hands comfortably positioned to your convenience; at your sides, behind your back, or across your stomach.

You can choose to count to 10, then start counting backward to 1. This will help your mind stay focused on the walking and not wander off somewhere else. If you are walking in a small space like your living room, when you finish walking in one direction, pause for an instant, and turn around deliberately and start walking again in the other direction.

As you put each foot forward, focus on the lift and the fall of your foot. Observe how the muscles move in your legs as you walk. Observe the movement and shifting of your body as you walk.

Your thoughts will go somewhere. Gently drag them back to the walking activity. Don't be frustrated with your mind each time it wanders off in some random thought. Pull its attention back gently to the walking.

When you are walking outdoors, observe everything around you and enhance the horizon of your view.

Focus on the sounds as you walk. Wherever you choose to walk, turn your mind's attention to the sounds you hear all around you. Simply observe the sounds without giving them any name or label. Don't categorize the sound as pleasant or unpleasant. Simply observe the sounds.

Next, focus on the smells. Again, do not be judgmental. Just notice all the smells you can sense and simply smell them.

Next, focus on the shapes and colors of the objects. If something else grabs your focus for a short while, gently bring back your thoughts to the shapes and colors of the objects as you walk. There is no need to be rigid or strict with your observation. Simply remember to focus on sustained awareness.

As you are nearing the end of your mindful walking exercise, again refocus on the physical aspects of walking including the lift and fall of your foot, the movement in your legs and body, etc. When you are ready to stop, pause for a moment and deliberately end the mindful walking technique.

You might start the walking as a purposeful act of mindful activity initially. As you practice with patience and commitment, you will notice that all your walking activities will be automatically converted into a mindful way of doing it.

Practicing Mindfulness in Your Conversations

Talking or communicating with people must be rooted in 'we' and 'us' and not 'I' and 'me.' Before we go into how to become a more mindful communicator, there are a few things that distract you from talking, listening and communicating effectively. Being aware of these elements will help you overcome them better.

We hear what we want to hear and not necessarily what is being said
Expressing emotions is always difficult
Lack of focus and attention
Jumping to conclusions before listening to the full talk
We are constantly busy
We prefer presenting our talk rather than listen to the other party talking
It is so easy to get trapped in divisive talks and mindless gossip
We forget compassion in our conversation
We are so caught up in our internal mind chatter that we cannot focus on what the other person(s) is saying
There are many more such reasons why we find it difficult to converse and communicate mindfully. So, why should we make an effort to communicate mindfully? Here are some benefits:
Mindful communication brings harmony and understanding in any relationship.

There will be more compassion in all your dealings with other people when you learn to listen and talk in a mindful state.

Mindful communication at work will help you collaborate better resulting in more effective solutions to problems than otherwise.

Talking to people in a mindful matter will help in resolving conflicts and ending unproductive arguments.

Mindful communication creates an environment conducive to transparency and openness in various business processes.

Tips to Communicate Mindfully

Keep Your Mind Focused on the Conversation – Being mindfully present translates to listening effectively to the person talking. Keep an open mind without making an effort to manipulate the outcome of the conversation to your end. Don't focus on the outcome of the conversation. Focus instead on what is being said among the talkers. Participating in a conversation mindfully also means you let go of outcomes. Holding on to expected results is what usually causes emotional outbursts resulting in noxiousness in the conversation.

Listen Mindfully – Listen to the words carefully that is being said by the person in front of you. When you listen mindfully, you are effectively putting yourself in the other person's shoes and looking at things from their perspective. Mindful listening includes empathy and trying to comprehend the underlying emotions in the talk. Mindful talking also requires you to look past the known flaws of the person talking to you.

Talking Mindfully – Choose your words carefully and slow down your speech considerably. One of the primary concerns that many of us encounter while talking is our inability to bring the mind's speed down to the level of talking speed. Thoughts run at super speeds and most often, unconsciously, we end up talking in an attempt to catch up with our thoughts. The ideal thing to do is to attempt to reduce the speed of your thoughts to the speed of your talking. This will help you choose words carefully and make sensible and meaningful conversations.

It is important to be conscious of every gesture and every facial expression you make. The goal of mindful talking is not to win but to present your perspective in a clear and unambiguous manner. When you watch people talk mindfully, you will notice no sign of fear, nervousness, or any kind of reticence in their manner. Yet, there will be politeness and compassion too when they articulate their thoughts. Mindful speech involves thinking before speaking.

Accept People As They Are – This is one of the most important aspects of being able to speak in a mindful manner with everyone. You must accept people as they are, unconditionally. You must accept the fact that all friendships and relationships will have cyclical ups and downs. There will be times when you feel sad and lonely and there will be times when the other people who are part of your relationships are feeling sad and lonely. Becoming unconditional friends means staying friends even if temporarily there are problems. It also means not to cling on to relationships despite knowing that some are simply not working.

Mindful communication takes a lot of practice. But it is easily possible to change from participating in a conversation mindlessly to becoming a mindful participant so that everyone gets value from the interaction.

Practicing Mindfulness at Work

How to be mindful and at the present moment on a busy working day when you are bombarded by emails, phone calls, presentations, meeting, and more. Here are a few tips to help you do this.

Be Consciously Present in the Moment – What does this mean? Suppose you have just finished a rather nasty call with, perhaps a colleague or a team worker, and you are now working on a report that needs to be submitted in the next couple of hours.

For the time you are working on the report, focus your mind completely on it. If your thoughts go back to that nasty fight you just had, acknowledge that the thoughts are there and gently bring back the focus of your mind to the report and continue working on it. It may appear simple while reading this tip, but it takes a lot of time, effort, and practice to become a master at this. Here are some ways you can attune your mind to get ready for mindfulness at work:

Make a decision at the beginning of the day to be mindful throughout the day. Take a few moments before you start the day to tell yourself of this intention to be mindfully present at each moment of the working day.

Work consciously. This could result in slowing down the speed of your working. But, in the long run, working consciously will prove highly productive

Be conscious of all the sensations while you work. Focus on your posture. Focus on the way the papers are arranged on the table. When you need to turn to the computer for something, focus on the movement of your neck, etc. All this will help your mind to remain on the job you are doing instead of floating around in other thoughts not related to the task at hand.

Pay attention to all the tasks you do including the mundane ones such as dialing a number on the phone, washing your hands, opening doors or even feeling your breath while in a meeting, etc. All these little moments of mindfulness will help make your entire day more mindful than otherwise.

Avoid multitasking – Multitasking is the act of doing two or more things simultaneously resulting in your mind having to shift its focus back and forth from and to the different jobs you are performing. Doing one task at a time focuses your mind on that task until it is completed. Actually, only a computer can multitask. The human brain at the cost of multitasking is madly rushing to and fro and losing control of focus.

Everyone now understands the non-productive aspect of multitasking. Yet, people indulge in it because they feel more productive. It is important to realize that multitasking cuts down on productivity and also results in less than optimum outcomes. Avoid multitasking and focus on one task at a time.

Use Reminders to Remind Yourself to be Mindful – One of the biggest problems we face while starting out on our journey of mindfulness is that we get so lost in our internal chatter and thoughts that we forget to be mindful. It might make sense in the initial days of your mindfulness journey to create reminders to remind yourself of your commitment to mindfulness. Here are some tips to set reminders:

Set a silent vibrating alarm on your phone

Put mindfulness on your calendar every day

Put some a small note or a small post-it on your computer to remind yourself every time you turn to your computer

Associate certain activities with mindfulness reminders such as meal times, meetings, or when you are shifting from one task to another, etc

Being mindful while eating or walking or talking or at work calls for a lot of work and efforts and patience. However, once you have achieved the way to do this, you will reap umpteen benefits including but not limited to a better quality of life with less anxiety and stress.

Chapter 6: Thoughts And Emotions

We get mixed up with our lives because we allow thoughts to take us into areas of our lives which may have been troubling. The moment that you step back in your mind to bad things that have happened to you, you step out of the current moment. That's not a mindful thing to do and in fact, you will be carrying all the baggage from the past into your present time.

Mindfulness is all about being present in the moment you are in. Thus, the exercises in this chapter are all about controlling the mind.

Learn about how your emotions work

Emotions only turn negative if you let them. What you need to recognize is that what gives energy to your emotions are just thoughts. When you feel a negative thought draw yourself back into this moment and examine what's happening in your life. Let go. The trick is trying to find a way to calm yourself and breathing exercises help. If it's a thought that hurts you, you tend to attach all kinds of emotions to the thought that create a chain reaction. If you react to a certain thought in a negative way, your subconscious records what is happening and every time you think the same thought, you will automatically jump into negative mode because your subconscious works quicker than your conscious mind. When you think a negative thought, create calmness by breathing properly. You teach your subconscious that those feelings don't create panic, anxiety or any kind of pressure upon you. Once you teach yourself this trick, you will find it easier to let go.

Breathe in through the nostrils, concentrate on the breath and then breathe out, making sure that the breath goes right down to your upper abdomen.

Learn to love yourself

People always back away when you talk about self-love. This doesn't mean that you always put yourself first or that you love yourself to the extent that you are always looking into the mirror. When you find that you are stressed and don't like yourself very much, you tend to make emotional mistakes because you don't care much about the consequences. Learn to respect yourself. You have to look at yourself and know that what you do in life is the best that you can do. One of the best ways of doing this is volunteerism. If you have any doubts about your abilities, you certainly can't doubt your sincerity and willingness to give if you are prepared to help someone out and expect nothing in return.

Volunteer to walk a dog at the dog shelter. Make a cake for an elderly neighbor or simply visit the neighbor and talk for a while. All of these things reinforce that you have value but remember you are not doing it to impress anyone else except yourself. Pamper yourself a little. This could be any kind of pampering, but what it says about you is that you do care about yourself. Thus, try something that makes your hair feel good or your skin feel great or indulge in a super bubble bath or sauna. If you don't love yourself or even like yourself very much, how do you ever expect anyone else to? What you need to do in this day is to make yourself worthy of love. That's what self-love is all about.

Share your love of life

There are times in everyone's life when it may seem like everything has gone wrong. Then something happens that suddenly lights up your day. You must have had this happen to you. I remember feeling like this and then being amazed as two little squirrels stood outside my kitchen door almost as if asking for something to eat. When you smile at people, you give them a mirror or positivity that bounces back at them and makes them feel happier too.

Mindfulness is all about being in the moment and in that moment you share a smile with another human being, you open up the path to someone else's happiness. Compassion is all part of mindfulness and a smile doesn't cost you anything at all but can lead you into more compassionate acts in the future.

In this chapter, we covered things that center upon emotions. These are not just emotions for others, but for yourself as well. When you feel self-love, you are able to give more of yourself to your enjoyment of life and do not have so many negative thoughts in your mind. That makes life a better place to be.

Chapter 7: Mindfulness Meditation Basics

While looking inside yourself with the idea of finding an untapped well of inner peace and tranquility might seem daunting at first, rest assured that it is something anyone can achieve if they dedicate time and mental energy to practice mindfulness meditation every day. What's more, after you get the basics down you will find that almost any situation easily lends itself to being mindful if you simply commit yourself to being fully present in the moment and open yourself completely to the signals that your body is sending you.

While one of the best things about mindfulness meditation is its malleable nature, when you are first getting started it is recommended that you set some time aside each day to specifically devote to the practice. Ideally, this should be someplace that is quiet and during a period of time when you feel relaxed and where you can devote as much as thirty minutes to going deep within yourself without fear of worldly distractions. Remember, being mindful is all about creating space between the sensory information that your body is always sending to your mind and your reactions to that information so the less stimuli you have to deal with at the start, the easier you will find the practice to be.

Getting started

Choose a set time and stick to it: As with any burgeoning habit, it is important that you create a routine for your mindfulness meditation and stay with it if you hope for the practice to stick. It typically takes 30 days for a new habit to take root in your daily schedule which is why it is important to commit fully to practicing mindfulness meditation if you ever want it to become part of your routine. Due to its low impact nature, nothing external is required, it is very easy for many people to make excuses to get out of meditating, especially if their daily schedule is already filled to bursting. If you find yourself always coming up with an excuse to get out of meditating in the moment, you may find the following piece of advice particularly useful. "Practice mindfulness meditation for fifteen minutes every day unless, of course, you are extremely busy in which case you should practice for thirty minutes instead." Don't let the outside world intrude on your potential for inner peace, find a time each day that works for you and stick with it no matter what; in a month's time, you will be glad you did.

Get started by focusing on the moment: While the ultimate goal of mindfulness meditation is to quiet the mind in an effort to find a state of internal calm despite the hustle and bustle of the outside world, many people find it difficult to achieve this state right out of the gate. Instead, you will likely find it easier to start to supplant any thoughts you might have by focusing all of your attention on the signals that your senses are relaying to you to the exclusion of everything else. While you might not feel as though you are receiving much data on the physical world, especially if you are practicing in a quiet, temperate space, the truth of the matter is that your brain naturally filters out approximately eighty percent of everything it receives, you just need to get in the habit of tapping into it.

With practice, you will learn to tune out your more common thoughts and to instead tune into what is going on around you. When you do this, it is important to simply take in the information your senses are providing without thinking about it too deeply or passing judgement on what you perceive. Judging tends to lead to additional thoughts or, even worse, comparison of the present group of situations to those of the past which is more likely to pull you out of the moment and make finding the state of calm you are looking for even more difficult than it is likely to be, especially when you are just getting started. Remember, the goal with mindfulness meditation is to get as close to existing in the moment as possible and ignoring everything outside of your current surroundings as much as possible. To reach the required state you are going to want to start by focusing on your breathing, the feel of the air slowly entering and exiting your lungs as well as any smells or tastes that go along with this practice. From there you can then expand the sphere of observation to any other sensations that your body might be experiencing, all the while going deeper into yourself in search of the point where your mind ceases to form new thoughts and simply exists in a state of peaceful relaxation.

Make an effort to avoid judging what you feel: When you first begin practicing mindfulness meditation it is perfectly natural for your mind to intrude with thoughts about your current surroundings or to fill the void you are trying to achieve with a constant stream of consciousness. This occurs because over the years you have trained your brain to constantly be moving from one thought to the next in a rush to reach some conclusion or another.

When you find these errant thoughts breaching your sense of mental calm it is important to not interact with them as much as possible and instead to let them simply float away without interacting with them. If you find yourself getting sidetracked it is important to not attach a judgment to what has happened and to instead simply center yourself once more and continue as before. While this step is the most difficult for many people, it is important to keep it up until it becomes second nature as any interaction with the stray thoughts, even if it is just to chastise yourself for getting off track is an easy way to let even more thoughts through which will make it more difficult to find the state of mind that you are looking for. Keep at it: When you first begin practicing mindfulness meditation it is important to do so with the right level of expectations regarding your results. Specifically, you will want to keep in mind that your mind is likely to wander frequently and that you will need to persevere through these periods if you are ever going to reach the level of mental quiet that you are looking for. To understand the ultimate mindset that you are striving for, you may find it helpful to consider the period of blankness the mind enters after a question has been asked but before the answer comes to you. Finding a way to reach this type of state is key to your long-term success.

When it comes to clearing the mind, some people find it helpful to visualize their thoughts as a stream of bubbles that they are watching flow past them; others visualize a gate coming down to block out the stream of consciousness entirely leaving the thoughts to pile up on the far side. While these visualizations can make it easier to be aware of stray thoughts without interacting with them it is important to not become too reliant on them as they are still thoughts and you ultimately want to do away with them once your mind has gotten used to the idea that it doesn't need to constantly be moving from one thought or another. However you manage it, it is important to not to worry about chastising yourself when stray thoughts do emerge and to instead simply acknowledge the lapse and then get back to what you were doing.

What to expect

While many of the benefits of mindfulness meditation include physical changes to the body, it can be difficult to track them without scientific or medical help. Instead, the first positive changes that you are going to likely notice are going to include changes to the mental conditioning you have been subjected too for your entire life. Living in a modern society typically leads to a desire to hide our flaws from others as well as ourselves and to treat uncomfortable thoughts and feelings in much the same way. This, in turn, leads to a desire to revise the truth and rewrite personal histories until they show things in a more flattering light. While not necessarily the most healthy way to handle issues, this common cultural habit is actually an offshoot of the instinctual primal desire towards flight or fight that help ancient humans avoid threats whether they were real or imaginary.

While it was this impulse that helped our ancient ancestors survive and thrive amongst harsh natural conditions, these days it is easy for it to instead lead to an undermining of the very traits and qualities that make us unique. This is perhaps mindfulness meditation's greatest benefit, it allows people to gain a deeper understanding of themselves which is the first step to a greater acceptance of both strengths and weakness and finding the best way to reconcile the two.

In place of this negative and potentially harmful mindset, regularly practicing mindfulness meditation can lead you to what is known as radical acceptance. Essentially it allows you to be more in touch with what you are experience and feeling in the moment without any of the negative filters imposed by society. Radical acceptance allows you to understand that just because you have the occasional negative thought or feeling doesn't mean that there is anything wrong with you and it is an amazing, and free experience. A major part of radical acceptance is embracing all of your firsthand experiences as they really are, something that learning to exist in the moment will make much easier than it otherwise might be. Additionally, you will find that you will soon have a greater tolerance for negative experiences, until you are ultimately able to let them occur without letting them impact your overall mental state.

This improved mental state comes as a natural side effect of learning to be nonjudgmental not just of your thoughts but your experience as well. Cultivating mindfulness means leaning heavily on the suspension of inner judgement which is a result of putting greater thought into your feelings, thoughts and reactions and why they make you feel the way they do.

Additionally, you will likely find that regularly practicing mindfulness meditation naturally improves your ability to be aware of your surroundings at all times, even when you feel otherwise occupied by specific thoughts or problems that you may be facing. Typically, most people are so focused on the mistakes they have made in the past or their plans for the future that they don't have any mental energy left over for the present. This is a precarious situation as it then becomes easy to miss out on all the pleasures of the present without even realizing what it is you are giving up in order to focus on the past which you cannot change or the future which is largely uncertain. Instead of existing in this mental fugue state, existing more frequently in the present allows you to strengthen your awareness of what is happening at any given moment, letting you take charge of your future in a more active way and banishing the specter of missed opportunities that so frequently hangs over the past.

This practice is what is known as meta-awareness which is a state where you are able to interact with your thoughts and feelings in a more objective and detached way. This, in turn, allows you to more accurately measure your experiences to determine how they are affecting your sense of self without the baggage that such things typically carry around with them. Essentially, meta-awareness allows you to view yourself in a detached and objective manner which can benefit virtually every aspect of your life.

Chapter 8: How To Apply Mindfulness Daily

There are many benefits of practicing mindfulness. Some of which include sleeping better, reduced stress and anxiety, improving concentration, focus, as well as confidence. It can also help to reduce fear and anger in your life.

Day to day our lives seem to be extremely busy. Often times we end up living on autopilot going to work, taking care of our homes, cooking our meals and taking care of our families. We feel that there are not enough hours in our day. Practicing mindfulness can reduce this panic and the feeling that there are too few hours available for us to do what we need to get done.

So you may be sitting there wondering how you are supposed to apply the practice of mindfulness in your everyday life? You need to understand first of all that absolute mindfulness is practiced by Buddhist Monks, those who have been taught the practice from birth. The good news is that you don't have to run off and become a Monk in order to apply mindfulness in your life.

Here are a few things you can do in order to apply mindfulness in your life starting right now. Incorporating these techniques into your daily life can help you stay fully aware and engaged in each moment of your life.

1. Remember that in order to be mindful you have to choose to be aware of each moment! You have to acknowledge that your mind is with you at all times and it is up to you to decide to keep it mindful of what you are doing and experiencing.

2. The first thing you should do each morning before you even get out of your bed is to take several deep breaths. Become fully aware of all of your surroundings and focus on each breath as you take them in through your nose and out through your mouth. Become aware of any sounds you hear as well as any smells you experience. Make an intentional choice to begin your day in a state of mindfulness.

3. You can also create a list of all of the things you are grateful for in your life. All of us face struggles in our lives, during this time if you are able to acknowledge the struggle but remind yourself of all of the things you are grateful for, you will see your stress levels reducing.

4. Begin focusing on your breathing! Many times when people begin feeling stressed they will begin holding their breath without realizing it. As you begin learning how to practice mindfulness in your daily life, start by focusing on your breathing. As you focus on inhaling and exhaling, you are becoming mindful of your breathing and you are focusing on the present moment.

5. During your day if you find that you are becoming stressed or overwhelmed, begin focusing on your breathing. Become mindful of your breathing and accept that you are in whatever situation you are in at the moment allowing it to pass. You will find that you will become much calmer very quickly.

6. Each day commit to spending 15 minutes allowing yourself to be still. Allow your thoughts to enter your mind acknowledging them and allowing them to leave. Do not allow yourself to become

anxious about any of the thoughts, just allow them to exist as they are.

When you start practicing mindfulness you will probably struggle with the practice for several days. Usually the first day is the hardest, but with practice you will find you have a greater sense of well-being in your life. You will find that you are calmer and able to focus more.

Chapter 9: Walk The Talk

If you don't do what you say, your children won't trust you. If you try to teach them something you don't practice, even younger kids will be highly suspicious of your motives.

Secondly, like it or not, kids model your behavior and your actions; mine certainly do. I have this habit of throwing my gym bag in the front hallway of our home before getting settled. My wife has mentioned that she'd prefer I put it away. I think that's a good idea, but I never do it. Now, I've noticed that my two kids throw their school backpack in the front hallway and I'm forever tripping on them! Am I a hypocrite for demanding they hang up their stuff ? Do I have any credibility here? Will their behavior change? No way!

So, the first step to teaching children mindfulness is to become mindful yourself. This really is mandatory. Good News! This doesn't have to be difficult or time-consuming. And the Good, Good News is that it will lead to health benefits for you.

Include Mindful Meditation in your Morning or Evening Routine

If you don't have a morning or evening routine, I highly recommend starting one. My morning routine has provided me and my followers with exponential happiness.

Here's my morning routine (as an example).

6:30 - wake up

6:31 - smile (even if I don't feel like it)

6:32 - spoon my wife (even if she doesn't feel like it)

6:34 - drink a glass of water

6:35 - meditate for 25 minutes

7:00 - 20 minutes cardio (I have my road bike mounted on a gizmo that allows me to ride indoors)

7:20 - weights and stretching

7:30 - COFFEE! Yes, my grand reward - it's usually a cappuccino

I do this every day, barring days I take my kid to hockey practice or when I'm ill.

Having a morning routine allows you to start your day strong and it will help bring out the best of you!

Mindful Meditation 101

Start with the basics

Sit in a comfortable chair or cushion and gently close your eyes. Keep your back straight, but comfortable. If you slouch, you will become drowsy and might nod off. Breathe normally without forcing your breath to be slow, fast, or deep. Think about the breath coming into the belly. Pay attention to the sensations of your belly expanding and contracting. Alternatively, you can focus on the breath in your lungs or as the breath passes through your nose. Choose what works best for you. NOTE: YOUR MIND WILL WANDER OFF. This is normal and it will always happen. In the beginning, or when you have a lot on your mind, your mind will spend more time wandering than focusing on your breath. Try not to be too hard on yourself. As soon as you notice that your mind has wandered, gently bring it back to thinking about your breath.

As an alternative, instead of focusing on your breath, choose to focus on things that you hear (and the silence between the sounds). Again, as you mind wanders, gently bring it back to this anchor - the sounds that abound.

I will shamelessly offer a plug for another book of mine if you want to learn more about adult mindfulness practice.

Click on the link below for more details...

Taming the Monkey Mind

Pay attention to the moments
We want your kids to live in the moment; not to dwell on the past or worry about the future.
Same applies to your thoughts.
During the day, try to pay attention to routine activities (eating, showering, brushing your teeth, driving to work...the list is endless). With time, you will more often than not, start paying attention with curiosity to your present moment experience. You will start paying attention to your kids' world too. And, those little details are where the joy is hiding!

Honestly, paying attention to your thoughts, emotions and your senses will unlock the door to a contented life.

Just tune into yourself throughout the day by asking the questions:

1. What am I thinking about?
2. What emotions am I feeling?
3. What are my senses telling me?

That is all you can think about...ever.

Learn with Kids

Participate in mindfulness exercises with your kids. You will find that, almost by osmosis, you will adopt a more mindful existence.

Chapter 10: What You Need To Know Before Teaching Your Child Mindfulness

Mindfulness is something that even adults can have trouble practicing. It requires a lot of mental focus, but it is also a practice that becomes easier with time. This chapter will provide advice on how to encourage your little one to keep trying, as well as some obstacles that you might encounter and how to overcome them.

Tips for Teaching Your Child Mindfulness: Before You Get Started

#1: Try Mindfulness Yourself

We are our children's role models. If you are constantly yelling when you are upset or you shut down when emotions become overwhelming, your child will see that and mindfulness will be more difficult for them. You will also have a harder time encouraging them to practice mindfulness since it can be hard to do at first and you are not practicing with them.

To practice mindfulness on your own, start by scheduling 5-10 minutes for meditation each day. Find a quiet place where you can close your eyes and relax. Focus on your breathing, inhaling for a count of five and then exhaling for a count of five. Pay attention to how the breath makes your stomach inflate and deflate. If you find yourself distracted, release the thought without judgment and return your focus to your breathing. As time goes on, you will be able to focus for longer periods without your mind wandering. You can even extend the time beyond 10 minutes once you are comfortable.

#2: Be Mindful During Daily Activities

Over the course of a lifetime, the activities that you do on a day-to-day basis become second nature. For most people, this means that they start to carry out their daily responsibilities in a robotic-like fashion, sometimes letting their mind wander without giving what they are doing a second thought. Have you ever pulled into the driveway of your house and realized you don't remember coming down the last few streets? This is from driving the same way over and over again. The mind goes on autopilot—this is the reason that many accidents happen within three miles of someone's home.

Being mindful during the day simply means being present. It means that instead of letting your mind go on autopilot while driving to work or doing the dishes, you take the time to realize all that is around you. You notice the flower bushes by the park and hear the sounds of the dogs playing there, instead of tuning them out. You feel the way your muscles move while doing the dishes, paying attention to how the way you move your hand removes dirty spots from the dishes.

#3: Be Sure Your Expectations are Realistic

People who are familiar with mindfulness often associate it with feelings of calmness and relaxation. The idea of a quiet home is enough for any parent to consider practicing mindfulness with their children. You should keep in mind, however, that teaching your child mindfulness does not mean they will be quiet all the time. While you might notice a difference in the number of tantrums and there will be periods of peace, keeping your child quiet should not be the ultimate goal of mindfulness. The goal is to teach your child the skills that will help them become more aware of their experience, both internally and externally. It will help them learn that their thoughts are only thoughts—not something that they must listen to or judge. Though mindfulness can help, your child is likely to still exhibit what could be considered normal kid behavior—tantrums, whining, arguing, and loudness—from time to time.

Overcoming Common Obstacles to Mindfulness

#1; Your Child Does Not Understand Mindfulness

Not only is mindfulness a big word, it can be a big concept to explain to a child. You cannot explain mindfulness to your child in the way that it has been described in these first couple chapters. Explaining it in a way that makes it seem complex will make your child feel as if they are unable to understand the idea. Without understanding it, they will not be able to find the motivation to practice it.

Keep things simple by explaining mindfulness as awareness. You are teaching your child to be aware. Awareness is feeling things and understanding thoughts as they come, in the present moment. It is knowing what is happening inside of our bodies and minds right now.

#2: Your Child is Not Interested

Mindfulness is not something that you can just do. Even though mindful practice is meant to induce a state of relaxation, it can be difficult to get your child to be mindful when they are in the middle of a temper tantrum. It can also be hard to get them interested if they have had a long day at school or have been cooped up because they will have an excess of energy that will make it hard for them to become aware of their present moment.

If your child is not interested in mindfulness or seems to wound up, do not force it on them. It is important that mindful practice is related to positive emotions if you want your child to be motivated enough to do it. If they seem to be too energized, try practicing mindfulness after playing or other physical activity. If you do become frustrated, remember to keep your expectations in check. You should be practicing mindfulness for the benefits—not to achieve a specific outcome.

#3: You Are in the Habit of Tuning Them Out

Parents lead busy lives, but that does not excuse us from interacting with our child. When your child is talking about something that excites them, give them your full attention. Avoid checking the ping on your phone. If you do need to take a phone call, excuse yourself and then find them when you are done. Encourage them to share with you.

This does not mean that you should allow your child to be rude. There are appropriate and inappropriate times to talk. Teach them the habit of saying 'excuse me' to interrupt other people's conversations. It is okay to ask them to wait before you attend to them, but do not neglect to pay attention to them.

If interruptions are a problem, then get in the habit of setting aside time for your little one to share about their day with you. It does take more than five to ten minutes. Try to avoid doing this right after school, unless they initiate it. Some kids are excited to share after school, while others prefer to keep to themselves for a while and relax before sharing.

Chapter 11: Mindfulness Meditation And Buddhism

Anyone can practice mindfulness even without Buddhism; however, Buddhists cannot practice their doctrine without mindfulness. This is because in Buddhism, "mindfulness" is synonymous with meditation. More often than not, mindfulness denotes the practice of intentional awareness of an individual's thoughts and actions without judgment in the present moment. It is employed both to the thoughts and feelings of the mind and the actions of the body.

In Buddhism, mindfulness is deemed as requirement for one's development of wisdom and insight. In the Noble Eightfold Path, right mindfulness is the seventh path while in the Four Noble Truths, it is the fourth truth.

Right mindfulness is also called the Right Meditation. There are a number of forms of both mindfulness and meditation. For instance, mentally providing a verbal name or label to every in breath and out breath on a sitting meditation is an example of mindfulness. On the other hand, an individual does not necessarily need to conduct a formal meditation session in order to apply mindfulness. Mindfulness is applied through allowing the mind to focus on what transpires in the present moment and at the same time being aware of the usual "commentary" of the mind.

Furthermore, mindfulness is done any time without being required to sit in a corner. For example, an individual can be mindful of the sounds of the wind; of the sensations in his feet as he walks; or the texture of soapy water as he does dishes. This denotes being mindful what happens in the present moment and at the same time, being aware of the commentary of the mind.

Right Mindfulness (Samma Sati)

The Dhamma, according to the Buddha, is the ultimate truth of things and is directly timeless, visible, and calling out to be seen and acted upon. The Buddha claims that the Dhamma is always available to every person; thus, it is realizable within oneself.

Sati, which is translated as "mindfulness" is a mental faculty, which brings the experience field into focus and makes it available to insight. As mentioned in the previous sections, mindfulness refers to awareness, attentiveness, or presence of mind. However, awareness involved in mindfulness is extremely different from the awareness that an individual displays during the usual mode of consciousness.

While all consciousness requires awareness in terms of experiencing or knowing an object, the kind of awareness applied in the practice of mindfulness is at a special level. This level is referred to as the bare attention, which is a detached observation of what transpires within an individual and around him in the present moment.

During the practice of right mindfulness, one's mind is trained to stay in the present moment, being quiet, open, and alert while reflecting what is currently happening. This means that all interpretations as well as judgments should be suspended. Should interpretations and judgments come up during the practice of right mindfulness, they should be simply registered, then dropped.

The practice of right mindfulness is to take note of everything as it occurs. This is comparable to a surfer riding the waves on the sea. Right mindfulness is simply riding the changes in the events transpiring in the present moment. The entire practice is a process of coming back into the present moment without being distracted with thoughts and without slipping away.

Mindfulness employs a persuasive grounding function. It secures one's mind in the present in order to avoid slipping away into the past or the future with his regrets, hopes, fears, and memories. Without mindfulness, the mind would be similar to a pumpkin when placed on a pond's surface. It floats away and would only remain on the surface of the water. However, the mind founded in mindfulness is similar to a stone, which stays where it is and sinks into the water, reaching the bottom of the pond. Strong mindfulness allows the mind to stay focused on its object and goes into its characteristics profoundly.

Four Foundations of Mindfulness (Cattaro Satipatthana)

Right mindfulness is developed or cultivated through the four foundations of mindfulness or cattaro satipatthana, which is a practice involving the mindful contemplation of four objective spheres, including the body, states of mind, feelings, and phenomena.

According to the Buddha, the four foundations of mindfulness lead the only way to attaining purity, ending grief and pain, overcoming lamentation and sorrow, realizing of Nibbana (Nirvana), and entering the right path. These foundations are referred to as "the only way" or ekayano maggo, which entails that the attainment of freedom can only happen through penetrating the field of experience through the practice of the right mindfulness.

The contemplation of the body is one of the four objective spheres and applications of mindfulness. It is focused with the existence's material side. The other objective spheres are concerned with the existence's mental side. All four contemplations are required to complete the practice of right mindfulness.

In general, the body is the first contemplation sphere to be taken up although there is no fixed order as to what sphere comes first. The other three spheres may be taken up later when mindfulness is strong and clear enough.

Mindfulness Meditation in the Buddhist Context

Mindfulness meditation, based on Buddhism, has three central purposes. These include knowing the mind, training the mind, and freeing the mind.

Knowing the Mind

Most people spend their hours, days, or even their whole lives caught up with concerns, activities, and thoughts just because it is easy to do so. Indeed, a great number of people dwell in their thoughts and actions, mostly negative, instead of understanding why they operate the way they do. Most people are clueless with regard to their motivation, thoughts, and the nature of their feelings and reactions.

In mindfulness practice, the first step is to discern oneself in terms of what goes on in the mind, body, and emotions as well as the underlying tendencies that operate within.

Knowing the mind is a part of mindfulness practice, which is a simple discovery process. It does not involve judgments, but a meditative discovery that calls for stillness. An individual's level of stillness serves as a backdrop, which highlights what is transpiring. An agitated mind is easy to notice and does not call for too much stillness. Thus, discovery entails familiarity. For instance, being familiar with what an agitated mind is, translates discovery. It is knowing what the mind is and its effect on one's body. Discovery is becoming familiar with the emotions, belief, and thoughts are present.

The aspect of knowing in mindfulness is conscious and deliberate. A presence of mind develops when you know how something works. It is clearly knowing that you know. For instance, you and a friend are a part of an unruly crowd. Both of you are not caught up in the agitation of the crowd. If you have the knowing aspect of mindfulness, there will be a hint of recognition, say, a smile passing between you and your friend as you know that you are not caught up in the agitation.

When it comes to knowing the mind, you only focus on knowing instead of attempting to change what is happening. Observing the mind results in a relief and a radical change, especially for those who are inclined to always make something happen.

Training the Mind

The mind is a process. It involves a series of processes that interact with each other. Therefore, it is not static, but pliable and easily influenced. However, you can train and shape the mind. One significant part of the Buddhist's practice of mindfulness meditation involves taking responsibility for the activities and tendencies of the mind so it can work in beneficial ways. If you fail to take responsibility of your own mind, external forces will train and shape it. These forces include companions, advertisements, media, and other components of the society.

The best way to start training the mind is in compassion and kindness. When you start to explore how to be kinder, more compassionate, and more forgiving, you can avoid mental conflict with yourself, others, or the changes in your life. During the practice of mindfulness, mental conflict may be revealed, which can take the form of confusion, despair, discouragement, aversion, anger, or ambition. When you address conflict with another conflict, it will only add up to your suffering. As such, it is best to start training your mind in compassion and kindness towards yourself, others, and the changes in life.

In some cases, making too much effort during mindfulness meditation can result in a negative way. When there is too much effort, it is like escaping something, making meditation as an obligation or a penance. It also tends to measure every progress, which interferes with the true purpose of meditation. A remedy to this is to train the mind to become more at ease with the way things are. You can develop an ability to be comfortable or decompressed with what is transpiring instead of organizing the conditions of the situation.

When your mind is relaxed and experiences rest during meditation, it would be much easier to train it. You also develop mental stability or concentration.

By training the mind, you can promote the growth of ethical virtue, discernment, generosity, the capacity to avoid clinging, and courage. Buddhists usually choose a specific quality to nurture one step at a time.

Freeing the Mind

In the Buddhist practice of mindfulness meditation, it is important to train the mind to let go of clinging. Once you are done with the first aspect of Buddhist mindfulness meditation, which is knowing the mind, it will reveal where and how clinging is present. There are some painful forms of clinging, including holding on to desire, pleasure, ideals, possessions, people, judgments, and self-image. All these limit the peace and freedom of the mind.

According to the teachings of Buddhism, people can let go of clinging, and consequently, free the mind as well as the heart. In the Buddhist mindfulness meditation, the ultimate goal is to free the heart from shackles, constrictions, or barriers. This starts by taking small steps that result in a corresponding peace. The heart will be completely at peace when it is completely free. On the other hand, attaining complete freedom is not easy to attain. It calls for training and knowledge.

The three aspects of Buddhist mindfulness meditation -- knowing, training, and freeing the mind -- all develop together. Once you know yourself, it will be easy to train yourself as well as know the needs that should be let go. It will be easier to know yourself when you train your mind more. In addition, you will be able to let go of more wisdom and strength. Consequently, the more you let go, there will be lesser obstructions to understanding yourself. Ultimately, all these will make it easier to train your mind.

On the other hand, only few people care for the state of the minds as much as they care for their bodies, possessions, or clothes. Caring for one's body is an everyday task; however, few people realize that their minds also need regular care and training. In the Buddhist ways, knowing, training, and freeing the mind are ways of caring for it and at the same time having the goal of becoming free from suffering.

Chapter 12: What Is Mindfulness?

If I ask you how much attention or how often do you actually think about the things you are doing, what would your answer be? If you'll answer honestly, you would probably answer not often. And rightly so because most of the things you and I need to do everyday, every hour and every minute need to be automatic. If they weren't, you'd probably go crazy, not get much done, or both!

Take for example breathing. Can you imagine if you had to think about taking each and every breath just to continue living? Or how about driving your car – can you imagine having to always think about or being mindful about how fast to go, how to make a turn and when to do so, and when to slow down or brake? Do you feel what I'm saying? Going on autopilot – especially when it comes to many routine things in your daily schedule – isn't necessarily bad. It's bad when you extend the autopilot habit to things in life that are best done with awareness – or with mindfulness.

When we talk about mindfulness, we're talking about a way of paying attention to the stuff that's going on in your life and being able to see them clearly. Take eating for example – instead of just mindlessly going for those that are easiest to prepare or get, you can choose to go for healthier and more nutritious ones even at the expense of flavors and being inconvenienced.

Another good example of exercising mindfulness is choosing your social commitments. What I mean by this is not mindlessly accepting any and all invitations to join social events, gatherings and functions. Exercising mindfulness means evaluating each social invitation to see whether or not this will be most beneficial to you and your life purpose – or not. Can you imagine if you're not mindful about the invitations you accept – you could end up partying almost every night to the detriment of your studies or career!

One good way to remember what mindfulness is all about is the acronym ABC. "A" stands for awareness, which is all about being attentive to the things you do, think and say. "B" stands for being with the things you're currently going through or are experiencing, which means ditching the tendency to automatically do things that tend to aggravate challenging situations even more. Finally, the letter "C" refers to choices – making wise decisions by choosing wisely. This entails separating or distinguishing experiences from reactions. By doing this, you'll make better and wiser choices, which can lead to a more joyful, content and fuller life.

WHY MINDFULNESS?

When you learn to practice the art of mindfulness on a consistent basis, you can start to live life to the fullest by winning the battles against, depression, anxiety and stress that result from your hectic daily schedules, as well as from many of your life's challenges. Specifically, practicing mindfulness consistently helps you live life to the full by:

Enabling you to identify your automatic reactions to things that happen in your life and being able to manage them wisely;

Allowing you to manage and respond to your life's very complicated and challenging situations in more effective ways;

Giving you the opportunity to see your situations more clearly and objectively;

Become much more creative;

Helping you achieve balance among your life's numerous areas; and

Making you more resilient in the face of life's challenges.

Make no mistake about it – mindfulness is a very powerful and effective tool for winning your battles against depression, stress, and anxiety. Keep in mind however, that it won't eliminate the reasons for your depression, stress, or anxieties. Mindfulness is a tool that helps you manage those reasons – also known as stressors – very well so that you can enjoy great emotional and physical health.

Chapter 13: Exercises To Reduce Stress And Anxiety

In addition to the techniques I used, there are several mindfulness exercises that can be practiced independently or in combination to help reduce the stress you are feeling. I'm going to divide these exercises into three basic types—breathing exercises, meditation exercises and physical exercises.

Breathing exercises are the most common. They are by far the easiest to learn. The person simply inhales and exhales, paying close attention to each individual breath. Slow, deep inhalation through the nose will also saturate the lungs and your blood with oxygen. That intake of air will also help to slow your pace. A slow, deep breath tends to relax the body because slow deep breaths are most common when we are at rest.

Those deep breaths also begin to repair the damage stress causes an individual. As they lower one's blood pressure, blood will flow more freely through the body. Blood with greater saturation of oxygen will help cells repair themselves faster and more completely. This mimics the process of cell repair and regeneration we experience as we sleep.

To perform the breathing exercise, sit someplace comfortable and shut out all distractions. Begin by fully focusing on each breath. The rhythmic rising and falling of your chest as you inhale and exhale will soothe your mind. As you breathe, think just of the air as it enters your lungs and is then expelled. In doing this you will fully experience the moment.

These exercises serve as a precursor for meditation. The presumption that many people have is that meditation involves a long period of uninterrupted silence. This is absolutely incorrect. Even short periods of meditative thought can reduce the stress a person feels.

An ideal means of attaining a sense of calm while at work is through the use of guided meditation. Many websites focused on stress relief will offer audio downloads that you can listen to. The majority of these meditations are less than five minutes in duration and are specifically focused on relaxation and stress reduction.

In addition to the basic techniques of meditation and breathing, one can add physical exercises to reduce stress. Like walking, other light physical exercises will focus the mind and alleviate feelings of anxiety. Stretching is among my favorite quick exercises that diminishes stress.

To do this get up from your desk and reach your arms up, stretching your body towards the ceiling. As you stretch, your heart pumps more blood through your body delivering more oxygen and nourishing your cells. Pay close attention to how your muscles feel. We'll have more physical exercise tips later in the book.

Before we get to the specific five minute program, I want to take a moment to teach four physical exercises that you can practice at any time, but that will be part of the five minute program. These exercises are part of a Yoga discipline called Naam.

Proven to manage stress, heal diseases and reduce symptoms of depression and anxiety, Naam has gained in popularity. Some doctors have even advised some of their patients to give Naam a try before using the traditional medicinal approach to address mild symptoms of anxiety. Naam uses movements, stretches, breathing and meditation to help people find a greater sense of calm and focus. These are hand exercises that can be performed quickly at one's desk to usher in sensations of relaxation, confidence and intuition. Let's go through them in order.

Calm. When you need to limit stress you can relax yourself by putting gentle pressure to a point between your second and third knuckles on your middle finger. With your palm up, move your thumb towards your palm until you feel a soft, slightly indented spot on the inside of your finger. By applying gentle, but firm pressure here you will trigger the release of tension throughout your body.

Strong. Oftentimes, the strength we feel wanes when we are stressed. In those moments, we need to boost it back up. This exercise will enable you to eliminate the chaotic feelings that accompany stress and restore your natural feeling of mental and emotional strength. To begin, touch your thumb to the side of your index finger between the first and second knuckles. As you apply gentle pressure to this spot, you will feel a sense of mastery within your mind. Sit up straighter and adjust your posture to complete this movement.

Bold. Stress and anxiety evoke sensations of fear, which limit our ability to act in any situation. We want to counteract that fear with a sensation of confidence and self-assurance. Begin by touching the tips of your thumbs to the tips of your index finger, like you are making a circle. As you exhale through your mouth, push your hands away from you. Breathe in through your nose as pull your hands back to your chest. Continue the motion slowly until you feel invigorated.

Savvy. Stress and anxiety will also inhibit your ability to think things through. When you need answers, stress will lock you down and limit the creativity and intellectual rigor you can apply to finding a solution. Begin by touching the tip of your right thumb to the tips of you index and middle fingers. Then place those fingertips on your forehead above the bridge of your nose. With your left hand bring the tips of your thumb, index and middle fingers together the same way that you did with your right hand. This time touch the tips of your fingers just above your navel. Metaphorically, you are joining your instincts and intelligence to inspire creative, productive thinking.

Chapter 14: Freeing Ourselves From Identification

Hopefully, you've made it this far and are now wondering how all this ties together with mindfulness and living in the present moment. Perhaps you want some practical mindfulness exercises that will help you to accomplish this. Trust me, you'll discover all the necessary techniques. But first, let me invite you to consider the importance of ideas, philosophy, mindset, or whatever you want to call it. By reading books, like you are right now, you can discover one idea that might change the course of your life. For me, more often than not, it's not one particular technique that has the biggest impact on my life. It's the new ideas and concepts that I haven't thought of before. The purpose of this book is to give you at least one seed that can have a positive impact on your life.

The first thing to recognize when trying to free yourself from identification is to take time to learn about your ego, which we've talked about in the previous chapter. Take time to reflect on the concept of having an ego and also reflect on the different roles it might play in your life. Maybe you have a strong identification with a particular concept of who you are that is causing you pain and preventing you from living in the present moment. Perhaps your ego is unconsciously addicted to drama, recognition, playing the victim, or acting superior. Maybe your ego is ambivalent, both afraid of attention, yet wants to be recognized. The ego can play many roles. It's been formed through whatever circumstances you've been through and will act differently depending on the situation. By reflecting on your past behavior and becoming aware of your present thoughts and feelings, you can begin to see a pattern. A pattern for a lot of people is the fear of not being enough. This is, of course, the ego feeling this. If the person whose ego feels this achieves all their goals and dreams, but has not yet become aware, then this person will still be afraid of not being enough. It's a game you can't win with more. The ego will always feel a lack of something and it will seek completion, but never find it.

Knowing how your ego operates is the first step to becoming free from identification with the ego. The second step is to think of yourself as the awareness behind the roles that the ego plays. You are the person holding the camera and your ego is the actor. You're not trying to control the various roles that your ego is playing, you're simply watching. Chances are that you no longer have to "try" to stop the unpleasant roles that your ego is playing. When being aware, you simply stop and choose to act in a different manner. This concept can help you to stop indulging in anxious thoughts, anger, or unnecessary stress.

Stop Trying to Be Yourself

So when you're no longer unaware of the roles that your ego is playing. You might have a tendency to listen to the advice "be yourself". Can you see how the ego can creep back in even stronger when you're trying to be yourself? Your thoughts will try to figure out who yourself is. By creating a concept of who you are, which is based on thoughts, you're more likely to be offended by small things and your ego will simply play another role. Pull back the layers and realize that you're already yourself. You are the awareness of everything and you're already as complete as you can be.

Changing the Patterns You don't Like

Have found any ego-structure or pattern that you don't like? If so, what is this fear that is beneath the surface? Maybe you're afraid of what people think of you? Perhaps you're a people pleaser? Or maybe you're the opposite? Can you find the cause of this particular structure? If you're acting as if you had armour around you, what's the reason for it? Have you been hurt, left behind or trusting to someone who ended up breaking that trust? Whatever the pain is, this probably plays some part in how you're behaving currently. Learn the lesson from it but don't let it destroy your future happiness. If you're avoiding falling in love for example, because of a belief that everyone is a douche and will eventually end up breaking your heart, then you're supporting a fear that is not helping you. Yes, it could happen that your heart will be broken again. Will you be smaller because it? No, accept that it could happen, be okay with that outcome and stop being afraid of the pain this could cause you. In the next chapter, I will share an exercise that can help you to overcome a lot of the fears that might stop you from living in the present moment.

Chapter 15: Mindful Meditation For Commuting Stress

It's not common for people to commute 30 minutes or more to their jobs. Whether you commute by public transit or private car there are many stresses involved in commuting. Having to catch a train on time, or worrying about traffic jams and other things that you can't control start your day off on a very stressful note. And when you're finally done working there is a stressful commute waiting before you can get home to relax too. Some people commute an hour or more each way every day to work.

Carpools and rideshares can cut down on the expenses of commuting but they can add to the overall stress of the experience too. If you have a long commute you are already stressed before you even really start your day, and the unhealthy food and caffeine laden beverages you eat during your commute don't help reduce your stress level any either.

If you commute in your own car you already know how stressful dealing with road conditions and other drivers can be. Road rage is a real thing, and it happens usually because drivers are so stressed out that they are not thinking clearly. They end up acting in ways that they would never normally act if they weren't constantly on the edge of a stress burnout. Commuting can also cause havoc with your spouse and family. It's impossible to make commitments to drive kids to lessons or sports. You may end up missing recitals, sports games and plays because you were stuck in a traffic jam. Commuting is something that many people think of as something that they have no choice but to accept.

Mindful Meditation for Commuters

With Mindful Meditation your commute can change from a stress inducer to a stress reliever. The motion of the car or the train can be very soothing and can help you focus your thoughts and be more mindful. Here are a few different ways that you can use your commute as prime meditation time:

Smartphone Apps

It's true that smartphones are usually not very helpful when it comes to reducing stress, but if you use your smartphone to run one of any number of meditation apps your smartphone can become a very powerful meditation tool. You can use apps that will help you meditate by guiding you through specific meditations or you can use your phone to listen to soothing music or binaural beats that will make it easier to be present and achieve a meditative state. If you have a long train ride or you usually take the bus you can relax into a meditation instead of stressing about your commute. Meditation Oasis makes several great meditation apps that are available on both Android and iOS platforms. Some are guided meditations and some are just music appropriate for meditation but the apps are free and very helpful.

Being Present

Do you have a tendency to drift off or zone out while you are driving? Lots of people do. Those people are missing a great chance to practice Mindful Meditation. When you are driving you have the chance to really focus on the world around you. It's almost as good as being out in nature. You can roll your windows down to breathe in the fresh air. Listen to soft music or turn off the radio altogether and just be in the moment. See the world around you and the beautiful natural world that you are driving through.

Mindful Meditation for Work Stress

Probably the most consistent source of stress in modern life is work for most people. No matter what type of work you do, and even if you really like your job, there can be work stress. You spend the bulk of your time at work so dealing with co-workers, bosses, and the demands of the workplace can cause a lot of stress.

Schedules, changing relationships with co-workers, and the hectic pace of work all contribute to stress related illnesses that are so common these days. When you add in the additional struggle to juggle things like parenting and relationship responsibilities with your work responsibilities the stress can become overwhelming.

The environment that you work in can also add to the stress that builds up at work. Closed up offices with no fresh air and a lack of natural light, open offices with lots of noise and distractions, and workplaces where you need to be on your feet or sitting at a desk all day without a break can be very hard to take over a long period of time.

Add in things like irregular breaks and meals eaten on the fly and it's no wonder why work is such a major stressor.

Another factor in work related stress is toxic co-workers and bosses. It seems as if every workplace at least one toxic person who is determined to make everyone else miserable so that they can be the center of attention. Toxic co-workers sap your time, your energy, and your positivity.

They like to turn other workers against each other with gossip and innuendo and spend more of their time gossiping and scheming than working. They also usually come in late and leave early, and may be take long lunches and breaks as well which interferes with the ability of others to take their breaks.

Mindfulness for a Toxic Environment

When you feel trapped in a toxic environment but you can't immediately get out of the situation or the office if it's affecting the entire office there are some things you can do to stop the negativity from impacting you and your health. When you have to work in a toxic environment or with toxic people you can:

Take a step back. Breathe deeply and remind yourself that you are not the problem and you can choose not to let that negativity affect you.

Visualize that negativity rolling off of you the way that water rolls off you during a shower. You may not be able to avoid the negativity shower but you can choose to let it all go down the drain instead of clinging to you.

Create a positivity oasis for yourself. If you have an office, a cubicle or any kind of private space create a soothing oasis just for you. Hang up art that you find soothing and positive. Write positive messages to yourself on sticky notes and hang them up. Keep a plant or flowers in there to reconnect with nature.

Mindful Meditation at Work

Depending on what your work situation is it can be a little more challenging to practice Mindful Meditation at work but it's not impossible. Taking even a few minutes when you are stressed out to focus on your breathing, be present, and relieve stress can make a big difference in your health and in your state of mind. Don't be surprised if the quality of work goes up as your stress goes down through Mindful Meditation.

If you have an office all you need to do in order to practice a little Mindful Meditation is shut the door, turn the ringer off on your phone, and turn off the lights in your office a moment. But if you don't have the luxury of having your own office then it can be trickier to find a way to work some Mindful Meditation into your day. Here are some fail-proof ways that you squeeze in the meditation that you need to keep you calm, focused and healthy throughout the day:

Go Outside

In most workplaces it's perfect acceptable to take a short five-minute break. Take advantage of this by going outside once an hour for a breath of fresh air. Find a stairwell or an exit that isn't usually very crowded so you can have a peaceful couple of minutes. Even if it's raining or cold it will do you a lot of good to get outside in the fresh air after being in a stale work environment.

Take a few deep breaths, focusing on the sensation of your breathing. Let your thoughts wander, just keep bringing them back to your breath and the sensations in your body. After a couple of minutes you can go back inside with your mind and body refreshed by the fresh air and deep breaths. You really should take at least a ten minute break every hour if you sit down all day at your job. A walk outside will get your blood pumping and prevent health problems as well as getting rid of stress and anxiety.

Find a Hiding Spot

If it's not practical to go outside each hour find a quiet and dark hiding spot closer to your office that you can use as a place to go for a little Mindful Meditation. Try to find an empty office, or a corner that no one really uses. An empty stairwell or utility closet can do the trick as well. All you need is a place where you can sit or stand quietly for a few minutes and focus on your breathing. In a pinch you can always duck into the bathroom for a few quiet moments.

Create a Hiding Spot

If you can't find a hiding spot anywhere you can make your own. If you work in an open office environment where there is no privacy you can make your own quiet space with a sleep mask and some headphones or earplugs.

When you need a break put a little note on your desk or your chair asking not to be disturbed. Put on some noise canceling headphones or pop in some earplugs and put the sleep mask on. The mask will block out the light and the bustle of the office and the headphones or earplugs will muffle the noise.

Then you can drift into a meditative state of awareness for a few minutes, focusing on your breathing. Set a timer for five or ten minutes and when you're ready to get back to work you will feel focused and refreshed instead of stressed out and anxious. If you really need a moment you can always put your head down on the desk for a few minutes blocking out noise and light with your arms.

"My co-workers thought I was crazy at first when I put my head down on my desk like a child but when they started to see how much it helped me deal with stress and anxiety they started doing it too. Every single one of them that tried it told me they felt better after ten minutes of quiet desk time. " – Lucy B.

Meditate on Breaks

Another way to meditate at work is to use your break time to meditate. This can be either a short break or during your longer lunch or dinner break. When you are on a break if you can't find a place where you can get the quiet you need you can always go out to your car, or go outside and find a quiet place to site. Many workplaces have at least some landscaped trees or grass where you can go sit. Just getting out into the natural world will do wonders for your health.

On longer breaks you can also do things like go for a walk around the block, go to a park and sit, or drop in a local yoga center for a lunchtime meditation or even a yoga class. The important thing is that you use the breaks you are given.

Stop working through lunch or dinner. Don't give up your break to get one more thing done during the day. That time is time that you really need to decompress and quiet your mind. It's time that you can use to let go of all that stress and anxiety that has been building up all day. Make your health and peace of mind priorities by focusing your time and attention on them. Check out some of these real world ways that people found to get in some Mindful Meditation during their work time:

Chapter 16: Mindfulness Exercises For Self Control And Emotional Stability

To gain self-control, you can apply each of these exercises to your daily life. You can apply any of these exercises in any random order:

Exercise 1: Breathe Mindfully

This exercise is popular because it is one of the easiest and most direct mindfulness techniques to pull off. It is also very flexible because you can perform it at any time of the day or night and at any place. It also takes less time. However, you should not underestimate its power owing to its simplicity.

This exercise will effectively help you regain your self-control during times of pressure and stabilize your emotions. Here are the steps to perform it:

Start by closing your eyes: Your eyes are a great source of distraction to anything you do and to achieve optimum results while using this technique, you need to eliminate all sorts of distractions.

Take a slow deep breath: Take a few seconds just breathing in and holding your breath.

Slightly open your mouth and allow your breath to flow out of your body slowly.

Remove your mind's focus from anything that could be on your mind: eliminate your pending work, your unfinished projects, past experiences and thoughts. Just allow them to float freely with the air as it goes in and out of your body.

Pay attention to how the air goes in through your nostrils and inflates your lungs and as it flows out through your mouth. As you do this, you will start to recognize some feeling of relaxation in your mind and body.

Repeat this process: of breathing in and out slowly while paying attention to nothing but your breath for around one to two minutes.

Exercise 2: Mindful Observation

Another mindfulness exercise that is simple and easy to apply, but still highly powerful at helping you regain self-control is mindful observation. This technique helps you bond with, and appreciate the natural environment for what it is.

In most cases, as we go about our daily activities with myriads of thoughts and worries, we never take a moment to appreciate the true beauty of nature. Because of this, we never realize nature's powerful ability to change our lives for the better by making us calm, relaxed, and in complete control of ourselves.

Here is how to practice mindful observation:

Choose any natural object within your surroundings. This can be anything: an animal, insect, cow, a tree, the clouds, or the stars.

Focus on watching the object you have chosen for maybe a minute or two.

During this moment of observation, choose to focus on nothing but the object itself. Let go of any thoughts you may have, any emotion, and any worry.

Observe the object in complete silence and take note of every feature the object possesses and the purpose it serves. Engage in the observation as if you are seeing the item for the first time in your life.

Allow yourself to feel amazed and consumed by every moment of its observation.

Exercise 3: Mindful Awareness

This exercise helps you feel relaxed and in control of yourself, and appreciate the small things that happen continuously without your awareness or appreciation for the importance they have in your life. Here is how to practice mindful awareness:

Start by looking at events that happen every day or that occur multiple times in a day. Good examples are your door opening, your computer powering on, the working of your mobile phone, and so on.

Isolate every thought and just focus on the one thing you have noted.

Watch and allow your mind to question every aspect you may not have noticed before.

Allow yourself to comprehend the capabilities of the mind that put the workings of that object you are looking into action. If it is an activity you do every time, take some time to appreciate how lucky you are that you came to be familiar with the activity that you are undertaking instead of taking it on autopilot.

Finally, take time to appreciate the advantages it brings to your life.

Exercise 4: Mindful Listening

Another important skill you should learn is the art of mindful listening. When you lose your self-control, it becomes easy to lose perspective while listening; when you lose perspective, you rush into judgments. Mindful listening involves listening patiently without passing judgment.

As you will discover, this technique can help you relax, and can keep you from losing your self-control. Here is how to practice mindful listening:

Start by selecting a piece of music, preferably one you have never listened to before (a piece of unfamiliar music).

Pay attention to the music without letting yourself judge the music or the artist.

Focus on every word or the beats if you cannot clearly hear the lyrics. When your thoughts try to stray away from the music, acknowledge this is happening and gently (without being harsh or hard on yourself) divert your attention back to the music. The whole point here is to listen and be in the moment without developing a concept or being judgmental.

You can repeat these steps with other tracks or just practice this technique when holding a conversation with someone.

Exercise 5: Mindful Immersion

Striving hard every day to achieve whatever endeavor you may have can weigh you down and have negative consequences on your self-drive and emotions. Mindful immersion is a technique you can employ to solve this. This technique gears you towards feeling content with the present moment instead of working hard to achieve more and more.

By choosing to experience the activity, you can enjoy it and gain satisfaction from it instead of feeling pressured into doing more or achieving more.

Here is how to practice mindful immersion and make the best of it:

When you start doing any activity you frequently engage in, start by engaging with it on a physical, mental, and emotional level.

Observe and let your mind become involved in every step of the activity. Let your body feel every step of the process.

Try to get creative by inventing efficient ways to complete the task. This way, you will not just focus on finishing it, you will start enjoying the activity; this will enhance your mood. When you start doing this, you will start gaining confidence in the work you do, which will boost your self-confidence and make your emotions stable. By working this way, you may achieve better results.

Exercise 6: Mindful Appreciation

This technique helps you recognize the simple, seemingly irrelevant, but vital things that support your life: the simple things you need to be thankful for and show gratitude towards. Being grateful of these things will help you stabilize your emotions because it will open your eyes to your many blessings, which will ensure you stop whining about almost everything that happens in your life.

Here is how to practice mindful appreciation:

Start by taking a notepad, paper, or use a note-taking app on your phone.

Take time to observe at least five things in your life that are extremely essential but you constantly take for granted because of your insatiable hunger for greater things in life. Moreover, take note of the things you possess that other people do not have. This includes things like skills and unique abilities.

Make a list of these things.

Next, ask yourself about things like what led to creation of these things and the purpose they serve in your life.

Imagine what a world without them would look like. Find as many reasons as you can about why you should appreciate the value these things provide in your life. By doing this (if you remain constant), you will start finding satisfaction in the things that exist in your life and you will realize just how lucky you are. This will improve you self-drive, mood, and emotions.

Exercise 7: Mindful Walking

A number of thoughts and worries can haunt you when you walk. Learning the simple skill of mindful walking can help you keep at bay worries that cause negative emotions and feelings of low self-esteem. Fortunately, this method requires very little effort.

Here is how to practice mindful walking:

Start by standing upright and adopting a still posture. Take time to feel the weight of your body as it presses down on the ground. Pay attention to the small bodily movements that are helping you remain still.

Bring your focus to the present moment. Keep away stray thoughts that may act as distractions.

Start out with the left foot. Narrow your focus on how it swings and how it feels as it hits the ground.

Repeat the same with the right foot.

Try keeping a slow but steady walking speed and try keeping your attention from wondering. You will find that this small exercise will help you keep away stray thoughts that challenge your self-control and emotions.

Chapter 17: How To Meditate As A Busy Person

At the present time, busy people find it hard to get relaxed. Though lots of activities like yoga are there which can help them in getting relax, the deficiency of time does not allow them to do such activities. Moreover, people use antidepressant tablets to get relaxed. Though antidepressants give a sense of relaxation, they can be highly hazardous afterwards. In such cases, meditation can be highly helpful as it helps in augmentation of emotional, spiritual and material levels. Meditation has been carried out since long and is highly fruitful of busy people. Meditation helps in lessening the stress and thus acts as an antidepressant. Moreover, those who carry out meditation with a proper routine have strong emotional health and get their stress reduced.

Meditation- Briefly Defined

Meditation is a procedure of mental exercises the augments the activities of brain and heart. The brain thinks in a better way and the heart results in better emotions.

Working of Meditation

The process of meditation works with our consciousness. Our brain is actually having four parts. Each part works separately. The separate working results in stress and pain. When the whole brain starts working altogether, the stress and the obstacles in your success eliminates. You are more focused and motivated to your goal and get your job done successfully. During Meditation, you make your all neurons work together. The complex development of brain results in deep thinking and brain works properly.

Short Period Meditations

Meditation is not a time taking exercise; you can do it for minutes to get relaxed mentally and physically. If you do meditation for ten minutes regularly, you will get great benefits emotionally and spiritually. Moreover, if you spend few minutes daily in meditation you will get your skills developed and improved. With the passage of time your meditation state becomes easy to achieve. The best time for meditation is early morning. The fresh air and environment in the morning can greatly help in short term meditation. Moreover, in the morning, your mind is completely at ease and the home environment allows you to meditate. You just have to leave your bed 30 minutes earlier than the others to get the state of meditation. This will even help in the homes where kids do not allow you to meditate. Once you achieve success in doing meditation, it will be much easier next time.

You can meditate everywhere

It is difficult to focus on something however you can meditate even on the move. It generally happens that people cannot find time to meditate early in the morning and rush to their offices to start working. For such people, a meditation on the move can be highly helpful. You can meditate everywhere even at your work desk. You can also meditate at a public place and can get rid of the noise of the public as well. You can use earplugs at public places to cut out from the public noise for few minutes.

Steps involved in short term meditation

Personalization: If you are a busy person and always remain under your boss, you can use the personalization technique of meditation. The best thing that you can do is the usage of personal pronouns. Do not copy the words spoken by your boss, do command or repeat them in your own words. Try to give new phrases to the instructions to give. Meaningful wording can be highly helpful in this regard. Using your own words, helps you improve your emotional health. Moreover, you get your spirits improved.

Enjoying the book so far? Leave a review!

Localization: It is common that when you struck among several issues, your attention diverts every moment. You cannot concentrate on one thing easily. However, you can meditate if you localize yourself. You have to sum up you all energies and focus on the major issue that you currently face. Make a list of issues and list them with priorities. Ponder over the problem that is listed at the top. This way, you can think clearly about the specific problem you face and get the solution early.

Memorization: Memorization greatly helps in getting the state of meditation. You just need to sum up the ideas in your mind and recall them at the time you need them. For some, the memorization is quite difficult. However, they do it differently. They like to writer whatever they want to be recalled. Doing so greatly helps in recalling something. Better memorization involves high-lightening the written idea. You can use pink, yellow or sky blue highlighter to give levels to the ideas. The pink idea is, of course, stands at the top. The high-lightening increases the chances of memorization three folds.

Verbalization: It is good to repeat the things you want to memorize. Repetition is considered key to success. If you use your verbal action to repeat the activities you want to do, you will get your mind sharpen. Your will power energizes to get the state you want to be at. Murmuring can be highly helpful but it must be clear to you.

Visualization: Whatever you visualize, you get it. You mind and heart together visualizes the ideas. The idea that you visualize hard to practice will surely be a hard task for you. However, if you consider something a piece of cake, you get the job done in few minutes without getting in any kind of hassle. You can practice by making images in your mind. The better the image the better will be the result.

Actualization: Whatever you do, values you. The actualization of the idea can be highly helpful successful for you. In case, you have done all the steps: personalization, localization, memorization, verbalization and visualization, but not the actualization your whole meditation practice goes spoiled. Practice whatever you think or verbalize.

However, you have to understand the seven Ps formula of meditation if you remain busy throughout the day.

Purpose: you must have purpose for meditation

Prospect: The prospect gives you direction to success

Place: a specific place is a must for meditation

Period: you must set a specific period of meditation

Preliminaries: Get relaxed and remove all that tightens you

Position: The body posture helps in getting better meditation state

Practice: Practice is the only step that worth all. If you don't practice all the Ps go wrong.

Chapter 18: The History Of Mindfulness

When you first heard the word "mindfulness," what crossed your mind? Did you think about long periods of quiet, motionless meditation? Well, you probably know there is so much more to it than just sitting on the floor and doing nothing.

After all, everyone has been raving about it - from A-list celebrities such as Emma Watson, Kobe Bryant and Angelina Jolie to highly successful entrepreneurs such as Arianna Huffington, Russell Simmons and Oprah Winfrey.

What is mindfulness really all about? What makes it so appealing not just to these famous and massively successful people, but also to the everyday office worker, stay-at-home parent or busy college student?

In this chapter, we will explore into the deeper meaning of mindfulness as well as how it came to be. You will also get to find out how and why it helps you get in touch with your true self.

The Meaning of Mindfulness

When you come to understand what mindfulness meditation truly means, you will feel a deeper sense of belonging to it. In other words, your perception of it will transcend its surface-value, which is the utilitarian role of helping you to unwind and melt away the stress. Therefore, by getting to know its deeper values, you will find that it is not just an option; it also has an integral part of your daily life.

The generally accepted definition of mindfulness is that it is a mental and emotional process. Specifically, it is the practice of focusing one's thoughts and feelings towards what is happening during the present moment. It is also widely believed that, through the practice of mindfulness meditation, one's ability to focus on the present moment can be strengthened.

Buddhist Beginnings

In Buddhism, the concept of our modern-day understanding of "mindfulness" came from the ancient Pali word "sati," a term that means "to bear in mind" or "to remember" (Pali is an ancient Prakrit language that is used as the liturgical and scriptural language of Theravada Buddhism). Traditionally, sati means to bear in mind and recall the dharma, or the teachings of the Buddha.

Ancient Buddhism further explains that you can understand the process of focusing on the present moment by learning the skandhas, otherwise known as the Five Aggregates.

The Five Aggregates organize your mind's ability of consciousness as influenced by your own pre-conditioned attitudes and past experiences. They are namely the material form, feelings, perceptions, and volition, sensory consciousness.

The Material Form is your physical body and the material elements that surround you, as well as enter and leave your body (such as the air you breathe).

Feelings are the emotional sensations that may be described as pleasant, neutral, or unpleasant.

Perceptions are your sensory awareness of the dimensions of an object, such as the color, shape, size and smell.

Volition refers to the mental, physical and verbal behavior you choose to conduct.

Sensory consciousness is your awareness of the thoughts that occur in your mind and the stimuli that your five senses can take in.

Buddhists explain that these Five Aggregates come in waves as one practices mindfulness meditation. However, you must avoid "clinging" to any of these five aggregates, so you can free yourself from suffering and unleash your true self.

Psychology

In Psychology, mindfulness may be regarded as a practice that can develop the mind's metacognitive abilities. Psychological researchers Kirk Warren Brown, Richard M. Ryan, and J. David Creswell explained that how a person defines mindfulness depends on who that person is and how mindfulness is applied.

According to them, some regard mindfulness as a mental state, while others describe it as a set of skills and strategies. Thus, there should be a clear line between the trait and the state of mindfulness.

Another psychologist, Scott R. Bishop proposed that mindfulness can be defined as a type of "non-elaborative, non-judgmental, present-centered awareness" wherein every thought, sensation and feeling that comes up to one's conscious attention is "acknowledged and accepted as it is."

Brown, however, explained that mindfulness is a quality of consciousness that manifests in – but is not necessarily the same as – the activities through which it is enhanced (such as meditation).

Steven F. Hick, the author of Mindfulness and the Therapeutic Relationship, explained that there are both formal and informal practices of mindfulness. The formal practice is mindfulness meditation, which involves the process of focusing one's attention on sensations, breathing, the body, or anything that takes place in the present moment. The informal practice of mindfulness is when you apply mindfulness in everyday exercises, such as being mindful while doing the dishes, eating, or listening to music.

Jon Kabat-Zinn, who is one of those responsible for bringing the teachings of mindfulness to the west, explained in an interview entitled "Underneath the Surface" his working definition of mindfulness. He said that mindfulness is "the awareness that arises when you intentionally pay attention to the present moment in a non-judgmental manner."

He further explains that the present is the only moment we ever really have "to be alive in," yet our attention to it is usually neither vivid nor stable. However, by training the mind to pay attention through mindful meditation, we can strengthen our ability to sustain our attention moment by moment.

How Mindfulness Meditation Came to Be

Following is a brief overview on the historical development of mindfulness meditation. By learning about its roots, you can appreciate the practice even more and this will hopefully inspire you to incorporate it into your everyday life.

Mindfulness meditation, as it is today, is founded on the vipassana meditation of Buddhism. The term vipassana means, "to become aware of the present moment as it really is." The practice of vipassana is meant to help one see the true nature of reality, which is the impermanence of things. By becoming aware of impermanence, one can break free or be liberated from desire, which is the true cause of suffering.

In fact, mindfulness is so important that it is actually the seventh step in the Noble Eightfold Path of Buddhism. To have the right mindfulness is to be conscious of what one is doing in the present moment and never be absent-minded. It is to be aware of the impermanent state of one's body, mind and feelings.

The person who is most responsible for spreading vipassana meditation throughout modern Asia and the West is the Burmese Theravada Buddhist Monk Mahasi Sayadaw U Sobhana (1904 – 1982). His publications and teachings became so widespread that they enabled him to help train over 700,000 meditators. His publications, along with accessibility to the Buddhist sutras, were translated into English, causing the concept of mindfulness meditation to become even more widespread.

A major proponent of mindfulness meditation in the west is Jon Kabat-Zinn, who created the Mindfulness-Based Stress Reduction or MBSR program at the University of Massachusetts in 1979. Kabat-Zinn is Professor of Medicine Emeritus and was a student of several Buddhist teachers such as Seung Sahn and Thich Nhat Hanh. What made his teaching of mindfulness appealing to the west is his ability to synergize it with science. As a result his stress reduction program was widely accepted in hospitals and other medical centers.

The movement that Jon Kabat-Zinn started quickly picked up pace and led to the Mindfulness Movement, which has led over 20,000 chronically ill patients as well as a great number of individuals in peak health to practice mindfulness meditation and allowing them to enhance their quality of life. Thus, mindfulness became a well-known mainstream concept and practice.

Naturally, the history of mindfulness goes much deeper than this, and it is up to you to discover the rest of the story. However, for the time being, let us move on to the next chapter, which discusses the benefits that one can gain from regularly practicing mindfulness meditation.

Conclusion

Despite its bad rap, it is important to recognize that many Type A traits are healthy and can work well for the individual. The combination of some of these behavior patterns can in fact be a recipe for success. A conscientious person who is a high achiever with strong leadership skills may make an amazing leader in business or any other pursuit. However, if achievement equates with a tremendous amount of stress in your life, then it can lead to physical and emotional disaster. If you have strong Type A tendencies and believe that you are out of balance in your life as a result, you need to actively seek ways to cope with these challenges - it could save your life.

To realize true joy, you need to appreciate the power of the mind. For thousands of years, scholars and scientists have tried unsuccessfully to fully understand the mind and this tremendous power it has to re-direct, restore and heal us. It is deceptively simple but true nonetheless, by making small changes in your attitude, you can alter your life. Rid yourself of any skepticism and brush aside all pre-conceived notions. Focus on improving your quality of life by embracing this time-tested art of mindfulness.

an advocate of alternative medicine once said, "Every time you are tempted to react in the same old way, ask if you want to be a prisoner of the past or a pioneer of the future".

So while you celebrate the drive and ambition that fuels you – use the tool of mindfulness to smooth out those jagged edges so you can then celebrate your success with health and longevity, peace and fulfillment, and a cheering squad of family and friends who are truly in your corner.

Thank you for downloading this book – I hope that you have found some valuable tools here to help you on the way to complete mindfulness.

www.ingramcontent.com/pod-product-compliance
Lightning Source LLC
Chambersburg PA
CBHW072012070526
44583CB00015B/1449